THE IMPOSSIBILITY
OF KNOWING

THE IMPOSSIBILITY OF KNOWING

Dilemmas of a Psychotherapist

Jackie Gerrard

KARNAC

First published in 2011 by
Karnac Books Ltd
118 Finchley Road, London NW3 5HT

British Library Cataloguing in Publication Data

A C.I.P. for this book is available from the British Library

ISBN 978 1 85575 824 7

Edited, designed and produced by The Studio Publishing Services Ltd
www.publishingservicesuk.co.uk
e-mail: studio@publishingservicesuk.co.uk

Printed in Great Britain

www.karnacbooks.com

CONTENTS

ACKNOWLEGEMENTS AND PERMISSIONS

First and foremost, this book is a tribute to the many patients who have taught me so much and, at the same time, have brought me closer to the "impossibility of knowing". I am grateful to each and every one of them, not only to those who are alluded to in this book by way of clinical vignettes, but also to those who have contributed so much to my psychoanalytic experience.

My thanks are also due to Brett Kahr and to very many of my dear colleagues from the London Centre for Psychotherapy, without whose support and encouragement this book could not have become a reality. Thanks, too, are due to David Mann, who encouraged me to contribute to his edited books and has given permission for two of the chapters to be reprinted from books he has edited.

In particular, Mrs Helen Plaut, Mrs Mildred Forrell, Dr Rob Hale, Professor Rosine Perelberg, Professor Joan Raphael-Leff, Professor Paul Williams, and Mr David Riley have been formative contributors to my capacity for not knowing. I owe an enormous debt of gratitude to each of them.

Finally, to the person I cannot thank enough—my husband, David, for his enduring love, encouragement, and patience.

Permissions

Chapter One
Lyrics quoted from "I Am A Rock" Copyright (c) 1965 Paul Simon. Used by permission of the publisher: Paul Simon Music.

Chapter Two
An earlier version of this chapter was first published in *British Journal of Psychotherapy, 10*(4), 1994.

Chapter Three
An earlier version of this chapter was first published in *British Journal of Psychotherapy, 19*(2), 2002.

Chapter Four
An earlier version of this chapter was first published in *British Journal of Psychotherapy, 13*(2), 1996.
    Also published in D. Mann (Ed.), *Erotic Transference and Counter-transference: Clinical Practice in Psychotherapy* (pp. 29-41). London: Routledge, 1999. Reproduced by kind permission of the publisher.

Chapter Five
Ten lines of "Daddy" from *Collected Poems*, by Sylvia Plath, reproduced by kind permission of Faber and Faber Ltd.
    Originally published in D. Mann (Ed.), *Love and Hate: Psychoanalytic Perspectives* (pp. 196–205). London: Routledge, 2002. Reproduced by kind permission of the publisher.

Chapter Six
An earlier version of this chapter was first published in *British Journal of Psychotherapy, 26*(1), 2010.

Chapter Seven
Originally published in *British Journal of Psychotherapy, 23*(2), 2007.

Chapter Eight
Extract from *Four Quartets*, by T. S. Eliot, reproduced by kind permission of Faber and Faber Ltd.
    An earlier version of this chapter was first published in *British Journal of Psychotherapy, 26*(3), 2010.

ABOUT THE AUTHOR

Jackie Gerrard is a Senior Member and Fellow of the London Centre for Psychotherapy and a Training Therapist and Supervisor for the LCP and other psychotherapy and counselling training organizations. Her background is in social work, and she has been a practising psychotherapist for almost thirty years. Her private practice is in Hertfordshire, where she sees individuals and couples for therapy and supervises trainees and qualified therapists. An important focus of her working life has also been on teaching and writing.

Introduction

I have found that, over a period of nearly thirty years working as a psychoanalytic psychotherapist, and for much of that time having been blessed with enough creativity to write many papers (most of which have been published), the theme permeating my work is that of my *subjectivity*. Thus, I have assembled those papers that illustrate this in the everyday and developed them into suitable chapters for this book. I believe that it is my humanity and subjectivity that give my patients a very particular experience in my consulting room, as, indeed, I am sure it is for many of us who work psychoanalytically. At the same time, we constantly face patients who expect us to "know" and, indeed, may initially come for analysis for that very purpose. This book is an endeavour to address the question of what it is that we try to offer our patients (and supervisees also) as, of course, we very rarely do "know".

I am sure that I, like many of my colleagues, started my training eager to learn and to know, and I have subsequently spent the years post qualification learning that I do not "know", cannot "know", and, indeed, should not "know". My stance here has been reinforced by the writing of the late Nina Coltart, who also stressed the significance of what we do not know (1992a, 1993). I hope it is clear that by saying I do not "know", I am continually endeavouring to hold a state of mind that can tolerate remaining open, bearing uncertainty, and avoiding, wherever possible, omnipotence and omniscience. Instead, offering an open and questioning mind and the wish to help patients to discover love in their lives (see especially Chapter Four) is what lies at the core of my working life. Many years ago, a patient who felt grateful to me at the end of our work together, wrote a final letter in which he said, "thank you for everything—and for teaching me that the answer is that there are no answers". I felt pleased with this outcome.

Parsons (2000) quotes from Barratt (1994), who contrasts the "computational" analyst to the "engaged" analyst, reflecting differences in the ways an analyst might make use of his mind in the psychoanalytic process. In short, the "computational" analyst would stress the use of his working ego (one mind acting on another), while the "engaged" analyst emphasizes the shared process between two people and the importance of making use of one's whole self (Parsons, 2000, p. 190). Parsons seems to align himself with the "engaged" analyst, but cites the danger in advancing one method against another and stresses the need for "holding the apparent opposites together in a creative tension" (p. 191). Although it is attractive to align myself with the "engaged" analyst, I, too, must emphasize the need to hold this "creative tension". I hope that, in the papers I have selected for this book, I have demonstrated that I frequently approach my patients from the stance of the "engaged" analyst, while endeavouring not to lose sight of the importance of my theory and training. In Chapter Seven, I explore, in some detail, what constitutes an "enactment" and what the outcomes, both positive and negative, can be from these "blind spots" (or moments of "losing sight") that occur in the analyst.

All my writing has been triggered by aspects of work in the consulting room and the dilemmas that have emerged for me in terms of response and interpretation. The task is usually determined by how to process my "affective response" (King, 1978) to my patients.

Each chapter outlines a particular kind of psychopathology and, for the analyst, the difficulties of working with these.

I have used, interchangeably, the words "analyst" and "psychoanalytic psychotherapist", and hope the reader will forgive this. My thinking attempts at all times to be psychoanalytic, irrespective of how I refer to myself.

The book is divided into three sections, and, although these are somewhat loosely formed and, indeed, there are considerable overlaps, for the sake of order and clarity I think it may be useful.

Part I centres on patients with specific types of psychopathology who pose particular difficulties for the analyst in forming a working alliance.

Chapter One focuses on work with obsessional and phobic patients and the obstacles they present to the work. It is named "On travelling hopefully", both as a metaphor for all psychoanalytic work and also, in particular, in relation to one patient who was phobic about travel. It is derived from the first paper that I wrote and published, way back in 1989, and so the title reflects my own journey.

Chapter Two outlines what Balint (1955) has named ocnophilic and philobatic types of relating: briefly, those who cling in their relationships and those who seek distance between themselves and their objects. Each places a certain pressure on the analyst by way of response. This chapter, like each chapter in the book, draws freely on my work in the consulting room and specific experiences with patients.

Chapter Three relates to "special" patients and, as well as my own clinical material, I offer two supervised cases to demonstrate my point. The task of working with people who feel themselves to be "entitled" is very tricky indeed. These patients are usually highly narcissistic, and probably those of the "thin-skinned" variety (Britton, 1998). Towards the end of this chapter, I delineate the differences, as I have understood them, between privation and deprivation and how this translates into " entitled" patients and those who consider themselves "an exception" (Freud, 1916d).

Part II is concerned with relationships where love, hate, and the erotic are a focal part of the psychoanalytic encounter.

Chapter Four has proved to be a seminal paper in my working life. I examine in depth the various aspects of loving and love in the consulting room and suggest that, unless a patient can evoke something of the analyst's love during their work together, whatever is achieved at the end of an analysis is lacking in some vital way.

In Chapter Five, I expand on this theme, as I felt that I had omitted to include a most necessary ingredient—that of hate. Both the analyst's hatred and love would need to be activated at various times for analysts and patients to have a full experience of human passion. Naturally, I draw on the theories of Winnicott, as well as Bollas and others, to offer various clinical examples that demonstrate the extremes of feelings that arise in the consulting room.

Chapter Six continues with thoughts on the erotic, but focuses on working with the omnipresent (Oedipal) themes of seduction and betrayal. I stress that these themes are a particular feature when working with the hysteric. Here, I posit the need for moments of a successful seduction to occur in the analyses of many patients, and I make a link with the earlier paper on love, where I stressed our patients' need to elicit their analyst's loving feelings.

Part III defines some particular, and rather extreme, challenges to my analytic work.

Chapter Seven (referred to above in relation to the analyst's "blind spots") focuses on enactments in the countertransference, but also concentrates on the rescue fantasies that can become activated in the analyst, especially when working with patients who demonstrate a hysterical personality. (In this, there is a link with Chapter Six.) It differentiates various types of enactments, such as through fantasy, action, use of words, and sexual response, and explores the particular rescue fantasies at work with patients who could be termed "hysterics".

Chapter Eight has taken as its theme the absent patient, and the focus is on "work" with a particular patient whose absences are prolonged, so that over many years of analytic work, she probably attended only one quarter to one fifth of her available sessions. The frustrations of the analyst, which can obstruct thought, are explored, and the struggle to discover meaning, in what seems to be a miasma of meaninglessness, is described.

The final chapter sums up some of the dilemmas facing us as psychoanalytic psychotherapists today, both in and out of the consulting room. It demonstrates "the impossibility of knowing", and I cite a personal vignette of my initial interview for training by way of setting the scene. Following this, I illustrate from clinical material some of the "human" (yet insoluble) dilemmas that have faced me over the years. The writing of papers and the writing of this book itself are just more of these difficulties that continually offer themselves to us, not just as to how to conduct ourselves as psychoanalytic psychotherapists or analysts, but also how to offer the human touch, where the need for just "being" seems far more important than the need for "knowing".

PART I
SPECIFIC TYPES OF PSYCHOPATHOLOGY

On travelling hopefully: some aspects of the difficulties of working with patients with obsessional thought disorder

"To travel hopefully is a better thing than to arrive and the true success is to labour"

(Stevenson, 1878)

This chapter examines the difficulties for the analyst in working with patients who are heavily defended by obsessional thought patterns and, thus, do not have the psychic freedom desirable for analytical work. Their capacities for fantasy and symbolization are impaired, and they have not been able to approach their therapy as a space for "travelling hopefully". Patients with obsessional thought disorder are generally recognized to be a particular challenge to the psychoanalyst.

The obsessional patient, because he seems to be powerfully defended against psychotic breakdown, finds it very difficult to play the "analytic game" according to our rule book. That is, he is normally censoring and controlling, in a way that does not allow space for fantasy, symbolization, and, of course, play.

This "space" I have called "travelling hopefully", and why I have done so will become clearer from the two clinical vignettes below. If these patients cannot fulfil their part in the task of analysis, then, by continuing to try to do my part, am I at best working too hard and at worst reinforcing their passivity and masochism in their object relationships? Through a better understanding of the literature on early damage, particularly with regard to "autistic barriers", I was helped to modify my technique and expectations.

George

George was twenty-eight years of age when he first consulted me, some years prior to the writing of this paper. He presented principally with what he called a travel phobia. He could not drive anywhere at all with a passenger in the car, and even driving himself short distances gave rise to a good deal of anxiety. His fears behind this "phobia" related directly to the accessibility of a toilet, and, in the event of one not being available, he was terrified that he would lose control, shit himself, and be seen by others as "weird". He showed a marked lack of spontaneity with me, a strong tendency to be in control, and there was a lack of response to, or interest in, me as a person. I was "The Therapist" to whom he had been referred.

By the second session, it was clear that his thinking was concrete: all was in terms of the known and nothing unknown could be played with, imagined, or fantasized about. George was a man with typical anal characteristics, also confirmed when he brought me his first cheque—typed, handed over in advance of my giving him an account, precise and pedantic.

Early on in our relationship there were some changes; he lost some of his dread of going out and met and stayed with his first serious girlfriend (and, indeed, his first sexual partner). The driving problems somewhat abated in that he began to drive and travel with his girlfriend. However, he was still presenting me with two areas where he felt totally stuck. The first was his job, in which he felt denigrated (as he did by his father), unfulfilled, and unrecognized. The second was his total inability to leave his parental home and consider moving in with his girlfriend. Any efforts on my part to get him to fantasize and play with ideas about moving met with a sheer block. He could not imagine. When he actually travelled he would not set out to an unknown destination without a map, so all would be precisely known in advance. In therapy, there was no travelling hopefully with new thoughts or ideas and, because there was no map available, there could not be a journey.

Thoughts from theory

Fenichel (1945) wrote of the shift of emphasis from acting to thinking: "Thinking is preparation for action. Persons who are afraid of actions increase the preparation . . . they also prepare constantly for the future and never experience the present" (p. 298).

This patient would seem to have replaced his primary love object (mother) with his house, and is now so fixated on this house as the means to his security and his identity that leaving it brings terror on all fronts. With me, the "labour" that cannot be undertaken is the journey through the labyrinths of his mind, where fantasies with regard to changing jobs and leaving home reside but may not be tampered with. They are all classified as "unknown" and, therefore, untouchable.

In addition to his obsessional personality traits, George suffered from the type of psychosomatic character disorder McDougall refers to in her paper of 1974, "The psychosoma and the psychoanalytic process".

> The ego, instead of detaching itself from external reality, may create another sort of splitting, in which the instinctual body is not hallucinated but denied existence through psychic impoverishment. . . . The result then may be a super adaptation to external reality, a robot-like adjustment to inner and outer pressure which short-circuits the world of the imaginary. This "pseudo normality" is a widespread character trait. [p. 443]

I was also helped by Miller (1983), and her descriptions of what it is that happens to the infant that leads to the creation of the false self personality:

> In obsessional neurosis . . . the mother's (or father's) scornful reactions have been introjected. The mother often reacted with surprise and horror, aversion and disgust, shock and indignation or with fear and panic to the child's most natural impulses. [p. 109]

This is also discussed by Bacal (1987) in his paper, "Object relations theorists and self-psychology". He examines the work of some of the British object relations theorists and describes Guntrip's *Central Ego*, "which tries to conform to the requirements of the outer world, sacrificing spontaneity and creativity to achieve security" (*ibid.*, p. 89). Bacal, quoting Winnicott, says that the false self . . . "is completely at a loss when not in a role and when not being appreciated or applauded" (Winnicott, 1960a, p. 150). "Winnicott regards the applause as the acknowledgement of the person's existence, which the false self cannot otherwise feel" (Bacal, 1987, pp. 92–93).

George frequently felt annihilated by non-recognition, reportedly at work, and, more significantly, within our sessions. Bacal writes of the "highly organised reaction within the self to the failure of self objects" (p. 95).

McDougall (1974) lists several factors observed in seriously ill psychosomatic patients, some of which George displayed: unusual object relationships notably lacking in libidinal affect, an impoverished use of language called "operational thinking"; *a damaged capacity for creating fantasy* to deal with infantile and present-day anxieties (p. 444). She writes of mothers who allow too much or too little psychic space. George suffered from a mother who failed by being too emotionally distant and, as a consequence, he became over-autoerotic. In other words, he could not depend on her for gratification, but only on himself.

As well as the part played by mothers (McDougall), Freud, in *Notes Upon a Case of Obsessional Neurosis* (1909d), writes of the father complex as playing a significant part in the founding of an obsessional personality, and, in particular, the fear of castration by the father. George came to me already, to some extent, aware of his fear and hostility towards his father; once in therapy, this became much clearer for him. He had many violent dreams where his father, or father-type figure, was the victim. He also brought a childhood memory of lying in bed trying to hold his tongue down in his mouth, in case his father should come in during the night and lop it off!

Freud (1909d) stresses the domination of compulsion and doubt in obsessionals. George, however, defended against areas of doubt (travelling hopefully) by constantly refusing to enter, either physically or psychologically, the spaces where doubt may occur. His internal situation was so full of doubt that he experienced the wish on my part to get him to fantasize as a threat and an aggressive intrusion into his mind, adding to the doubt with which he already felt burdened.

In Freud's words, "an obsessive or compulsive thought is one whose function is to represent an act regressively" (*ibid.*, p. 245). For George, thoughts replace action; actions and new thoughts imply doubts (about love and hate, security, identity) and, therefore, cannot be contemplated, and *his* thoughts need to blot out *my* thoughts. Continuing analysis of this state of affairs for George only brought about his agreement and helplessness that it is so. To quote from Fenichel, "The fear of any change from the known present condition to a possibly dangerous new state makes patients cling even to their symptoms" (1945, p. 298).

George's fears grew in leaps and bounds when he thought his girlfriend might accidentally have become pregnant, and we understood that his rage with his parents increased markedly at the time his mother was pregnant with, and subsequently gave birth to, his sister when he was four. *There are to be no more babies*—a deadening, murderous attitude both to real babies and also to my creative thoughts (see also Britton, 1989).

I also used theories of symbolization and autism to try to understand this patient. Plaut (1966), in his paper, "Reflections on not being able to imagine", poses the hypothesis that the capacity to form images and use them constructively is dependent on the individual's ability to trust. Failure in this, which reflects a failure in ego development, "impoverishes life and requires careful transference analysis in order to further the ego's function to trust, both in relationship and in one's imagination" (p. 147)

Klein, in her paper, "On symbol formation" (1930), concluded that if symbolization does not occur, the whole development of the ego is arrested. I feel that perhaps it is the other way round, as Plaut suggests, that is, *first* the ego has to develop to a point where symbolization can occur. Segal differentiates between early symbols (which she calls symbolic equations) and later symbols, with their characteristics of imagination and representation. An example of a symbolic equation is when Klein's little patient, Dick, sees pencil shavings on the floor and says, "Poor Mrs Klein" (p. 33): to him, the pencil shavings *were* his therapist. It is the later symbols, those that enable imagining and representation, that are missing in this patient. Segal (1957) connects the "capacity to experience loss" with the ability to make use of symbols freely. "The symbol is used not to deny, but to overcome loss" (p. 395). In the depressive position, if all goes well, the capacity to symbolize is used in order to deal with the earlier unresolved conflicts by symbolizing them. If this does not happen, the conflicts and anxieties of earlier times remain and prevent healthy growth.

Klein's patient, Dick, is interested in trains, stations, door handles, and the opening and shutting of doors, and Klein felt these "autistic objects" and this autistic behaviour was about the "penetration of his penis into mother" (1930, p. 29). Dick was unable to bring into his fantasy life his sadistic relation to his mother's body. Here is a recent dream from George's material that illustrates this.

> My house was on fire, but didn't seem to be too dangerous—nothing was really getting burnt. I went into my parents' room—they were doing morning-type things (Dad was shaving or reading the paper). The fire was burning above them but not in their room. They knew they would have to leave the house but there was no urgency. Then the scene changed to me and Mum in the breakfast room. I was getting some explosives ready and Mum was encouraging me. I fired them into a broom cupboard. Then I went out of the house with Mum and Dad to get the car out of the garage. However, I remembered I'd left some evidence of the explosives, which the Fire Brigade might find, and so I went back in to get rid of the evidence. They were shaped like Italian bread sticks and called *broden*.

The fire the patient produced seemed to separate Daddy from Mummy, and then he could show Mummy that he, too, had explosives to fire. If he can fill her tummy with his faeces/penis then she will not have any babies from Daddy, only from him (and he will not have to face his exclusion and separation). Perhaps I am the Fire Brigade, who may find the evidence if he is not careful. George accepted my thoughts about the dream, but offered very little himself in the way of association, though he did confirm that the "broom cupboard" was very much seen as Mummy's cupboard.

I read with interest Tustin's book, *Autistic Barriers in Neurotic Patients* (1986), which started to make some sense for me of aspects of my patients. The fears Tustin describes have been referred to by

George at various times in his therapy. These are: falling, being out of control, falling apart, spilling away, losing the thread of continuity which guarantees existence, threat of total annihilation, a state of being "gripped silly" and forgetting (*ibid.*, p. 192)

He struggled against all these fears to keep on going, to maintain an appearance of normality, and to develop perfectionist expectations for himself. The "insufferable catastrophe" in these autistic patients that Tustin describes, and in the autistic part of neurotic patients, is the experience of bodily separateness from mother (*ibid.*, p. 43) The result of this is that patients in encapsulated autistic states lack a sense of self and of individual identity. The primary psychic mishap leads to an obsessional need to feel in control of what happens and may also lead to phobic reactions (*ibid.*, p. 26). This is an accurate description of George.

Tustin finds that autism has been a protection against panic, which seems to increase as the autism diminishes. Tustin also makes a point about safety, which she calls the "rhythm of safety". This is a derivative creation of the baby's rhythms and the mother's rhythms while the child is at the breast.

The hope is for this rhythm of safety to be found in the therapy situation, arising out of a deep, reciprocal relationship. The autistic child's lack of a sense of safety is due to his feeling that he is not in absolute control of mother's body (as part of his own). Over and above his lack of control of her body, even less can he control her emotions. Autism is a technique to avoid becoming conscious of the "black hole" of separation, of partings, of endings, and, ultimately, of death.

Peter

Peter was an immature twenty-six-year-old when he consulted me for difficulties in sexual relationships. He described what I felt to be a very ambivalent, dependent relationship with his parents. He was effeminate, though heterosexually inclined, and was terrified yet desirous of an intimate relationship with a girl. He saw himself as undesirable and like a small child. He was highly obsessional, had bedtime rituals (which later abated somewhat), and set his thoughts, as they occurred to him, down on paper (to empty his mind). He would read a book, see a friend, view a programme on television, because his thoughts told him (compulsively) that this should be done. The task could then be ticked off his list. There was no conscious wish or ability to engage in pastimes and enjoy them for themselves. Initially, he used his sessions with me in the same way, for spilling out material that had to be got through. Having "vomited", he then felt temporary relief. (He used to vomit frequently as a child, running around the room, spilling it out everywhere.)

His mother suffered from a disabling disease and had been confined to a wheelchair since Peter was young. He was the only child. Both parents were overprotective to the point of being stifling. Using McDougall's model, while George's mother was too absent and so he became over-autoerotic, Peter's mother was too present, and so a healthy degree of autoerotism was not allowed to develop (i.e., he did not learn to depend on himself at all but always felt the need of an external object). The consequence of this is that Peter was now over-dependent on others for his sense of self, his security, and, as it felt to him, for his existence itself (see also Chapter Two, "Spaces in between").

His fears were death, space, and becoming an adult (as well as falling apart, being out of control, forgetting, breakdown, and spilling away). His defences were, outside the sessions, phobic anxiety and compulsions, and within the sessions, exercising control over me and using obsessional thought patterns. Again, the theme arose of not feeling free to "travel" or to contemplate a state of being where "the true success is to labour". Peter was hell-bent on "getting through" whatever he was engaged in. This might be the material he was bringing to the session, it might be a terrifying journey away from home, or it might just be a day at work. For him, too, there was no sense of enjoyment, no savouring of a chance to wander about, to imagine, or to play with ideas. He tried to control what I did, what I said, and what could be put into him. He censored and heard and felt what he chose to.

In *Notes Upon a Case of Obsessional Neurosis*, Freud tells us of his patient's obsession for understanding.

> He forced himself to understand the precise meaning of every syllable that was addressed to him, as though he might otherwise

be missing some priceless treasure. Accordingly he kept asking: "What was it you said just then?" And after it had been repeated to him, he could not help thinking it had sounded different the first time, so he remained dissatisfied. [1909d, p. 189]

Peter demonstrated the same trait in our sessions. He went over and over what I said until he managed to make it all rubbish and senseless (i.e., destroyed it). However, we also got to the fact that he relentlessly persisted with understanding and questioning because this was a diversion from feeling the pain of what is. "Why, why, why" is an escape from "it hurts like hell".

As Freud says, "the analysis of the obsessions . . . has already warned us to regard our patient's hostile impulses as particularly violent and as being in the nature of senseless rage" (*ibid.*, p. 190). Peter, like George, had violent dreams, and so let me know about his violent impulses towards both his parents (and me), although this knowledge proved to be of little benefit in his therapy. His task was to do battle with the analytic model and, thereby, me, and what I had to offer him.

I understood this to be more than ordinary resistance. Freud has described resistance as the name given to everything in the words and actions of the analysand that obstructs his gaining access to his unconscious. However, what both George and Peter demonstrated in their particular inability to "travel hopefully" was a terror of the analytic process due to its threat to their identity, sanity, and ability to carry on being (warding off total collapse).

In discussing how to work therapeutically with autistic patients, or those with a capsule of autism, Tustin (1986) says this needs to be done by first modifying the autistic barriers and then healing the damaged psyche. She also emphasizes the need to develop the capacity to mourn and to face their terrors, instead of avoiding them. She feels they need time and freedom from pressure and suggests that we show them how to wait by being able to wait ourselves until we sense the time when they can be helped to live a more normal life. (In Chapter Eight, "A question of absence", I have again stressed the need to wait.) I have used these ideas and feel more prepared to wait in my work with these patients, and sometimes very small shifts occasionally do seem to occur. For instance, Peter's parents went on holiday. Despite his fear of being left alone, he coped well for the week at home, *enjoyed* his freedom and the space he had for himself, and, although things were far from perfect, as his obsessional, ritualistic night checking increased, he came to me happier, satisfied with himself, and claiming that perhaps he did have "substance" after all.

* * *

George spent a whole session in tears (I could hardly believe it) following the sudden death of a loved dog and, although sad, he recognized that it was good to cry, that he was mourning a loss, and he felt more real. He wept when he wondered about the dog going to "doggie heaven", and somehow used an image of her face in the sky receding among the stars to deal with the gradual realization of her loss (using symbolization in the constructive way Segal (1957) suggests is necessary). In the next session, and the last before a summer break, he came saying there were two things on his mind—the dog and his forthcoming holiday. The memory of the dog was receding a little, he was less tearful now, but still missed her in the house and all her funny ways. The forthcoming holiday was something of an adventure, in that he was travelling to a new place with his girlfriend (having spent the past few years at exactly the same spot). He told me he was not dreading the journey nearly as much as in previous years; indeed, there were parts of it he was quite looking forward to (he seemed to be saying that since coming to see me he felt increasingly able to manage journeys). I wondered about the connection between the two things on his mind, the dog and the holiday, and I thought about separations. He immediately recalled a dream wherein a jazz pianist was playing music that was moving and evocative and was making him tearful. In the dream, George asked what the words were, and was told they were in the programme and written in German. German is the language he spoke in his usual holiday place—another way he could communicate. I felt that tears were also about having found another way to express himself. He recalled that some years ago, before he started therapy, he used to come home from work on Fridays and play the piano and could feel tearful himself about certain music—songs about wanting a loved one, or losing a loved one.

So, perhaps he found a language: I wondered if he could use the tears in a relationship to share pain and loss with me. The holiday, he insisted, was not a loss, there was still for him the appointment after the holiday, *the thread of continuity*, and this is what seemed vital for him. McDougall quotes the Simon and Garfunkel folk-song:

> I touch no-one and no-one touches me
> I am a rock, I am an island
> And a rock feels no pain, and an island never cries.
>
> (Paul Simon © 1965)

The struggle in sessions with both of these patients had been about my "touching" them. If I did, their fears were of facing weirdness and madness (total collapse), which constitute the pain of the rock and the tears of the island. Perhaps they feared that I, too, could not face this pain.

Incremental changes can occur, however, as we saw with Peter. But I am very conscious of McDougall's words when she concludes, "The stifling of feeling, the breaking of associative chains, the attack upon the analyst's attempts to make symbolic links may give the analyst the feeling that his patient is unanalysable. And it may be so" (1974, p. 458).

Conclusion

The question I have posed in this chapter, which perhaps remains somewhat unanswered, is, can an analytical approach with patients whose obsessional defences are so powerful and so deep-rooted reap rewards? Some developments in their therapy suggested that small shifts could indeed be achieved, but I had to accept that the journey would be a long and painful one and the ultimate destination might not be very far from the starting point. It is, indeed, a frustrating journey for the analyst. I was greatly helped by my understanding of the literature, as I have illustrated, particularly in terms of early damage and the need to be patient. Indeed, the theories supported my helping these patients to see therapy not so much as a complete rescue, or a total persecution, but perhaps more as something of a hopeful journey we could make together.

CHAPTER TWO

Spaces in between

This chapter attempts to examine ideas of space between
therapist and patient, using Balint's and Winnicott's thinking on space in relationships and its significance in the
consulting room. Vignettes from work with four patients are cited,
to bring my thinking to life. Here, the dilemma for the psychotherapist is what kind of space, and how much space is needed by the
patient, for the optimum working relationship.

When we consider the relationship between mothers and babies,
we know that some mothers leave too much space between their
babies and themselves and some are impinging and stifling. The
mother who sensitively teases out and tries to satisfy her baby's
needs is the one most likely to contain her child. Similarly, in the
consulting room, we therapists are striving to work with our
patients within the optimum space between us.

Balint's 1955 paper, "Friendly expanses—horrid empty spaces"
formed the basis of his later book, *Thrills and Regressions* (1959). It is
here that Balint first explores object relationships in terms of spaces
between them. People are divided into two types: those who need
objects and cannot live without them, and those who find them a
nuisance. To try to explain these two types of relating, Balint takes

for his model amusements found in fun-fairs, most of which, he says, are about thrills—those who enjoy them and those who do not. He coined two new terms for these two personality types. First, a "philobat", which is a person who enjoys such thrills. This is derived from the Greek *phil*, meaning love, and "acrobat", one who walks on his toes (i.e., away from the safe earth). The opposite of a philobat, a person who cannot stand the thrills of the fun-fair, is an "ocnophil", which is a person who prefers to cling to something firm or else his security is in danger. This is derived from the Greek *ocno*, meaning to shrink, to hesitate, to hang back.

The philobat is alone, relying on his own resources. The philobatic thrill, Balint says, comes from a heroic act and is a "symbolic representation of the primal scene and the forbidden incest" (1955, p. 227). His attitude to safety/mother earth is ambivalent: it offers security, but also provokes an attraction to danger. The ocnophil is also ambivalent. In danger, he will cling to a firm and protective object, but he also carries the fear of the object letting him down. It may not be so safe—it may even drop or abandon him. He clings as an expression of fear and as a defence against it. These two attitudes are by no means confined to the external world. They represent an attitude towards inner relationships and inner fantasied dangers:

> The ocnophilic world consists of objects, separated by horrid, empty spaces. . . . Fear is provoked by leaving the objects and allayed by rejoining them. . . . The philobatic world consists of friendly expanses dotted more or less densely with dangerous and unpredictable objects. . . . Whereas the ocnophilic world is structured by physical proximity and *touch*, the philobatic world is structured by safe distance and *sight*. [Balint, 1955, p. 228, my italics]

Both ocnophils and philobats have reacted to the traumatic discovery of the separate existence of objects (in the first instance, mother). Both are ambivalent towards their objects: the ocnophil mistrustful and suspicious, and the philobat superior and condescending. The ocnophil can destroy his love objects by too much clinging, whereas the philobat can destroy his by the use of too much superior skill.

Ocnophilia and philobatism, then, are secondary stages, the first stage being that of *primary love*, and hence Balint uses the word love (*phil*) to denote their origins. He dispenses with the term "primary narcissism", where there would be no relationship other than that to the self, and uses the term primary love instead, claiming there *is* a primary relationship between infant and environment. He states, "the aim of all human striving is to establish—or probably re-establish—an all-embracing harmony with one's environment, to be able to love in peace" (1968, p. 65). According to this theory, the individual is born in a state of intense relatedness to his environment: self and environment interpenetrate one another. They are "harmoniously mixed up". He gives examples of the fish and the sea (is the water in the mouth and gills part of the fish or part of the sea?); he also talks of the mix-up in the womb between foetus, amniotic fluid, and placenta (1968, p. 66).

At this point, we can move to Winnicott and see the similarities in some of his views. In his paper of 1952, "Anxiety associated with insecurity", he made the controversial statement "there is no such thing as a baby". He substantiated this by saying, "if you show me a baby you show me someone caring for the baby, or at least a pram with someone's eyes and ears glued to it. One sees a 'nursing couple'". Before object relationships, says Winnicott, the state of affairs is not an individual, but an "environment–individual set up". (Thus, he would seem to be in complete agreement with Balint's "harmonious interpenetrating mix-up".) Winnicott says that the centre of gravity of the being is not in the individual, it is in the total setup (1952, p. 99). The setup, Winnicott postulates, is initially created by the mother in her "primary maternal preoccupation". This mental attitude of the mother's "gradually develops and becomes a state of heightened sensitivity during, and especially towards the end of the pregnancy. It lasts for a few weeks after the birth of the child" (1956, p. 302). It provides a setting for the infant's constitution to begin to make itself evident, for its developmental tendencies to start to unfold, and to own its own sensations.

At the end of the stage where mother and infant are merged, Winnicott (1971) states, there comes into being "potential space" between the mother and the baby. In this two-person existence is the potential for *creativity, play, and cultural experience*. Potential space is the term Winnicott used for an intermediate area of experience between fantasy and reality. It lies between the inner world ("inner psychic reality") and the external world ("actual or external reality"). Potential space occurs, therefore, between the harmonious interpenetrating mix-up and before the development of the space in between (mother and infant). The baby is at a stage of separating out from the mother and the mother is lowering the degree of her adaptation to the baby's needs (*ibid.*, p. 126). In this stage mother and baby are *both joined and separated*. Winnicott asks us to hold this paradox. He says: "the baby's separating-out of the world of objects from the self is achieved *only through the absence of a space between*, the potential space being filled in the way that I am describing" (*ibid.*), that is, with illusion, with playing, and with symbols.

He argues that the mother (or analyst) needs to offer the opportunity for the baby (or patient) to move from dependence to autonomy, and claims, "where there is trust and reliability is a potential space" (*ibid.*, p. 127). In the potential space between mother and baby there arises creative playing, wherein use of symbols can develop—symbols that stand both for the external world and for that which relates to the individual. Winnicott, here, gives us his idea of a *third area of human living*: one that is neither inside the individual nor outside in the world of shared reality (*ibid.*, p. 129):

> This intermediate living can be thought of as occupying a potential space, negating the idea of space and separation between the baby and the mother . . . its foundation is the baby's trust in the mother experienced over a long enough period at the critical stage of the separation of the not-me from the me, when the establishment of an autonomous self is at the initial stage.

I will illustrate this with an example given by Ogden in his paper "On potential space":

> A 2½-year-old child, after having been frightened by having his head go underwater while being given a bath, became highly resistant to taking a bath. Some months later, after gentle but persistent coaxing by his mother, he very reluctantly allowed himself to be placed in four inches of bath water. The child's entire body was tense; his hands were tightly clamped on to his mother's. He was not crying but his eyes were pleadingly glued to those of his mother. One knee was locked in extension while the other was flexed in order to hold as much of himself out of the water as he could. His mother began almost immediately to try to interest him in some bath toys. He was not the least bit interested until she told him she would like some tea. At that point the tension that had

been apparent in his arms, legs, abdomen and particularly his face, abruptly gave way to a new physical and psychological state. His knees were now bent a little; his eyes surveyed the toy cups and saucers and spotted an empty shampoo bottle which he chose to use as milk for the tea; the tension in his voice shifted from the tense insistent plea: "my not like bath, my not like bath", to a narrative of his play: "Tea not too hot, it's okay now. My blow on it for you. Tea yummy". The mother had some "tea" and asked for more. After a few minutes, the mother began to reach for the washcloth. This resulted in the child's ending of the play as abruptly as he had started it with a return of all of the initial signs of anxiety that had preceded the play. After the mother reassured the child that she would hold him so he would not slip, she asked him if he had any more tea. He does, and playing is resumed. [1985, p. 130]

Ogden's observation shows us how there was an absence of the state of mind required for playing (i.e., potential space), followed by its presence. I shall move now to thinking about applying Balint's and Winnicott's ideas to the spaces experienced in the consulting room between therapist and patient.

Clinical examples

Jean

Jean was in her forties and was in twice-weekly therapy for some years. She told me that she identified with the Hans Christian Andersen fairy tale of "The mermaid". Briefly, the nub of the story is: the mermaid is the youngest of six daughters of the Merman King. Her mother had died when she was young and she was looked after by her father's mother. She is quiet and thoughtful, gifted, and has a beautiful singing voice. She takes an interest in the world above from what she sees below, mainly from shipwrecks. At fifteen, she is allowed up to see the world, and she encounters a prince on his ship and falls in love with him. In a storm, he falls overboard, and the mermaid rescues him from drowning and swims with him to a beach. She lays him down and hides and watches. He wakes up and sees another young woman, whom he imagines has saved him, and falls in love with her. The princess is devastated. Her grandmother tells her that the only way to gain an immortal soul is to be so loved by a human being that you are everything to him and he marries you and vows to be faithful to you for all eternity. Then the mermaid's body can become infused with her partner's soul.

The mermaid then goes to a witch and, in exchange for her beautiful voice (i.e., her tongue), she gets a potion to change her tail into legs. She returns to the prince, who loves her as a pet but he marries the girl from the beach whom he thinks has saved his life, and the mermaid is only the bridesmaid. Her sisters give her a dagger, to plunge into the prince's heart and so regain her tail, but she cannot bear to do this. Instead, she falls overboard and is transformed into a gentle wind, having to do good deeds to regain her soul.

Jean's identification with this story is that she felt she, too, had given up her tongue to try to win love. Her tongue was the instrument that would have expressed the feelings she had suppressed throughout her life. The story also tells us that there is a search for fusion, that is, "her body becoming infused with her partner's soul". So, her prior experiences were of non-intimacy, while her hopes and dreams were of an intense closeness.

She told me, somewhat in despair, that she had come to therapy for "the space in between". As she had also talked of wishing to find "the playroom", I assumed that prior to finding "the space in between", what she needed was for us to create together potential space. In fact, for Jean, there would seem to have been far too much space in between (more of a gulf) in her early life. Her needs derived from a felt lack in her early years of this potential space (where there is an absence of the space in between) where play could begin. I saw Jean, in Balint's terms, as taking a predominantly philobatic stance towards her world of objects (people). For instance, she would ring my bell, enter by seeming not to see me, fixed my consulting room door in her gaze, and, once inside, checked the environment for similarities and differences (a shifted ornament, a vase of fresh flowers—no changes in the environment I provided would go unnoticed). In contrast, she rarely looked at me and seemed hardly to see me. Her fears stemmed from a feeling that her mother never really saw or heard her, in particular after the birth of a younger sibling when she was three. Consequently, it was difficult to create an environment where we could really play together in an alive way. She saw me as "dead", and could not quite believe that in my mind she was very much alive. She could not allow me to be truly alive in her mind either. She seemed to adopt the philobatic attitude of superiority and contempt towards me. Jean created a somewhat safe environment out of the couch—once she lay down she could allow herself to snuggle into it and to close her eyes and permit and even enjoy silence. Sometimes, the silences continued for an extended period, and within it I experienced, not a space between, but a large gap, and even a gulf, which could grow ever wider between us. At other times, however, I felt I was the "good enough mother" who was facilitating Jean's thoughts and ideas, subsequently to be shared and worked on with me in a really creative play space. She was able to share her desires through the images that move her: those of closeness and intimacy—the harmonious interpenetrating mix-up that Balint writes of. In her images were the separateness/togetherness of Winnicott's theories. She spoke of a picture of a mother and child with heads held closely together. There was another of father and son walking down the street hand-in-hand. In both pictures heads or hands are almost fused; it was unclear where one began and the other ended. These were images that could move Jean to tears—two people held together in a special, intimate, almost symbiotic way. Something she had and lost very early in life, or possibly never had at all.

We sometimes had moments where she experienced this intimacy with me. One such moment was when she asked to borrow back a painting she had given to me, saying in a rather deprecating way, "I suppose it's in the file." I said that it was not in the file, and was able to find it immediately among my papers. Her eyes filled with tears, which I think were about how much she felt she really was held in my mind, and there was a sense of being very close. To mark this, she subsequently wrote me a beautiful poem, attempting to depict the "intolerable pain" of having no inner reservoir of previous experience of being held in mind in this way.

There was certainly flow and progression in our time together. Jean discovered her femininity and her sexuality. She slowly and movingly came to life, partly through discovering her aggression. Her image of herself and me together in the consulting room changed. Initially, we were two blocks with no movement. Later, we were depicted in a painting also as two blocks, but closer together, each with a hole in the middle through which ran a brown, curved, thick river. This could be a phallus; it could be an umbilical cord. It could be making us both women with a vagina, or mother with baby attached. Whatever it represented, we were closer to an inter-penetrating mix up that could well lead to potential space, as indeed it sometimes did.

Later, we had a very important breakthrough. For some months, Jean had an image of my flailing in my chair helplessly behind a newspaper which looked like a printed firescreen. From my right armpit a dagger pointed towards her. This meant that, for her, it seemed that I was hiding behind a blur of printed words (the books and theories that she feared stopped me from really seeing her). It also meant that she could not get close or my dagger would pierce her heart. (The mermaid has to plunge the knife in the prince's heart so that she may live again.) I think, in Jean's scheme of things, closeness meant the danger of one of us being destroyed. Prior to a holiday break, it seemed that some physical movements of mine led to some psychical movement of hers. I had left my chair to put on the fire for her when she felt cold. I had also left my chair to change the calendar page at her request. I think this enabled her to feel that I did have her well-being and needs in mind. After the break, she told me that the image had changed. It had reduced to the size of a keyring that she could hold in the palm of her hand. The knife had become a tiny plastic knife. Neither of us could damage the other with it. There was now nothing between us in her mind and she could look across at me and say, "Hello, Jackie Gerrard." (I refer to this vignette again in Chapter Seven, on "Enactments".) This mermaid had found her tongue and a new communication, with-out having to use the dagger! The telling of this created a very important closeness between Jean and myself, and we were both very moved by the telling.

Sheila

Jean's images of near fusion remind me also of Sheila, and the prob-lems for the therapist in dealing with a patient who is "in love". Sheila came for therapy at a time when her twelve-year marriage had reached a crisis because she had fallen in love with another woman. She was feeling both ecstatic in her new-found passionate relationship, and devastated at the idea of the break-up of her marriage and the possible loss of her three young children. She was a person who tended to relate in an ocnophilic way, terrified of too much space, experiencing expanses as unfriendly and uncontaining and looking for objects to cling to with an idea of their offering her safety. We came to realize that she had experienced a close, possibly stifling, relationship with her mother in the first two years of life until her younger sister was born. After this, mother seemed to switch her affection to the new baby, leaving little Sheila "out in the cold". It seemed probable that in her first two years she was not really contained and held safely, but was either overly impinged upon or was left too much to her own devices.

What emerged in therapy was the wish to be in a state of being "in love"—in a blissful union with another. Being in love offers the possibility of being merged, so the anxious, lonely "I" can become the ecstatically dissolved "We". One can shed anxiety, but the price is the loss of oneself. Yalom, in *Love's Executioner*, differentiates between "falling in love and standing in love" (1991, p. 11). Falling in love is a loss of one's self, while standing in love is retaining one's own completeness. This state of falling in love can drain life of its reality and put one out of touch with oneself. The danger of being alone, isolated, and separate does not have to be faced.

It seemed that Sheila's early experiences of a mother who frequently could not offer her the containment and space she needed propelled her into seeking her recent love affair. In the space between us, she had internalized our relationship. She had then been able to discover her own potential space, where she tried to paint and sculpt, and through these media she was able to depict her longing for symbiosis. She sculpted mothers and babies and drew many intertwining adult figures, as well as infants and adults in the womb.

Thus, both Jean, who used philobatic defences, and Sheila, who used ocnophilic ones, were, at heart, seeking the same basic relationship: a "harmonious interpenetrating mix-up". Sheila came to realize that an ocnophilic clinging did not actually offer her secure holding, and she was gradually able to let go of her husband and, to some extent, of the desperation for, and obsession with, her lover.

She worked hard in her therapy and, although the bliss and merging were "out there" with her lover, she internalized a lot of what I said and would often quote my words from a previous session. I think she found she could be contained by me and "held" by the analytic space, so that gradually her ocnophilic way of being was transformed into a greater use of potential space and an acknowledgement and acceptance of the space between herself and others. Clinging offers pseudo-intimacy. Sheila learned slowly and painfully to trust that perhaps she could attain real intimacy only when she could let go and stop clinging. That movement was accompanied by feelings of desperation and rage. Rage with the original mother, with her husband and lover, and, of course, with me. None of us could offer a perfect, containing environment for her.

John

John, in his late fifties, was in three-times weekly therapy with me. He came to me originally rather depressed, lacking enthusiasm for life, with obsessional traits reflecting a lack of spontaneity, difficulties in imagining or symbolizing, fears of intimacy, and a deep sense of shame. He had also lost his sex drive and was filled with self-hate. He said he had coped with life up until now "by fighting, denying, and being aggressive". This showed me how persecuted and threatened he felt by his objects. However, he had, unlike Jean, not managed to create a friendly, philobatic existence either. He was afraid of objects, had great difficulty in trusting, and yet, as a child, clung to his mother and, to some extent, his house, as his only hope of salvation from the persecutory world around him. But they continually let him down and abandoned him. To a large extent, for John, neither his objects nor the spaces in between were safe. Expanses were not friendly; they could contain horrid objects at any time, and so were more like horrid empty spaces. He, therefore, veered between ocnophilic and philobatic ways of relating. He had developed skills of wits and power in his work to attempt to negotiate his way in the world—a world almost devoid of trust. I felt that John rarely, if ever, experienced a "structureless friendly expanse" in his infancy. He had both the ocnophilic mistrust of, and the philobatic superior attitude to, his objects. It seemed not to have been possible for his mother to allow separation through play in a potential space between them.

Our sessions, too, lacked play initially. He planned what he would say in advance and even dream material was treated concretely, as opposed to symbolically. Over time, however, and also, like Jean, having managed to express his aggression towards me through some very angry confrontations, he came to trust me more. One of these confrontations arose out of an attempt on my part to renegotiate our fee. I had felt somewhat manipulated initially into accepting a lower fee than I had wished for. Over time, I became increasingly aware of my resentment towards John over this. When his material turned to issues of money and also to feelings of impoverishment, I was able to bring up again the question of my fee. I wondered if one of us had to feel as if he or she did not have enough—and perhaps it had better be me. He rushed to offer me a higher fee, but by the next session he felt furious: that he had been manipulated and betrayed by me. John felt that negotiation would be demeaning and hated me for bringing up the subject of money all over again, when he had felt it was settled and, thus, its meaning hidden from us. Eventually, out of this exploration arose memories of dealings with his mother and his feelings that negotiation could only lead to loss of face and personal humiliation. We did then manage to find a fee that was a compromise for us both, and I think a little trust was established, though we were to have several more confrontations during which John became very angry with me.

With an increase of trust came a noticeable letting go of his tight controls. His harsh superego softened somewhat, his sexual urge returned, and he slowly developed a little more self-liking. Together with all this, and towards the end of his therapy, came sexual fantasies about me. An early, remembered trauma was reaching out to touch his mother's naked body and getting his hand slapped. He said he wanted to relive this trauma and work it through with me. He related his sexual fantasies about me. However, he began to do this in such a way that it felt as if he wanted to turn the fantasy into a reality. He said he felt that I was hiding behind my professional mask, that I was being coy.

Originally, I felt that he had moved towards me, closing the earlier gulf that had existed, and making himself vulnerable by sharing these fantasies. For a time I felt we were truly in the area of play, of potential space where creativity and spontaneity were really happening between us. However, as I started to experience something persistent in the telling of these fantasies and his expectations from me, I imagine that I withdrew somewhat, recreated a gap between us, and wondered if we had not moved away from creativity and play space. In the very act of my wondering about this, and my concern about how not to slap his hand as his mother had done, I feel I moved away from participating in this potential space and turned (with his help) what had been between us into a gap, or even a gulf. (This theme is also explored in Chapters Six and Seven, with Sam.)

In time, we were able to overcome this hitch, and John and I were able to return to a space where we could play together. I think he came to understand that the sexual fantasies were something of a manic defence against the ending: that we were soon to be separated.

Shortly before the therapy terminated, John could fantasize about whether or not I would miss him and whether or not he was lovable to me. He seemed to allow himself to have value for me. I felt we had restored a potential space and that, one hopes, he took this "third area of human living" away with him at the end.

Peter

A fourth patient, Peter (also described in Chapter One), has been the closest to the model of Balint's ocnophil among any patients I have seen. When we met, he was twenty-eight, an only child of anxious parents and a mother who became handicapped soon after his birth. Peter clung to me and to his closest objects in the desperate hope that we would hold and contain him. I could not offer Peter what he felt he needed. His trauma seemed to originate in his birth, where his environment was radically changed because he became separate from his mother. Individual and environment were acutely felt as separated out. Tustin (1990) postulates that after birth a mother's mind can act as a substitute placenta, by which mother and baby become mentally attached to each other: "the mental connection of *understanding* compensates for the loss of the ever-present physical connection by the umbilical cord" (p. 82). If emotional connections do not compensate for the physical ones, the baby experiences overwhelming rage and distress. Newborn babies, she says, "need to be held in the 'womb' of the mother's mind" (p. 82).

Because of this very early damage, where Peter had not experienced being held in the "womb of his mother's mind" (or, in Winnicott's terms, "primary maternal preoccupation"), he was also afraid of the space in his own mind. He filled his mind continually with obsessional thoughts and ruminations that terrified him.

Peter avoided an awareness of the space between himself and me. He wanted me to know his every thought, feel his every feeling. He clung to me to counteract the lack of safety in a world that was constantly shifting and changing. At the beginning, he found our breaks very difficult indeed. I used to have to tell him where I would be going on holiday so he could look at the map and mentally put himself in the place where I was. We would not really be apart in his mind. Very slowly, he learnt to deal with our breaks and separations to the point where I could at least mention the possibility of an ending to the therapy. However, I suspected that after our ending, he would quickly try to replace me. He could not, in any way, rely on, or trust in, his own containing function. Tustin (1990) wrote of the need for "a relationship with a separate human being who is linked by caring concern for their welfare" as being "the only hope of a continuing sense of safety" (p. 139). Bick (1968), in her paper on skin, described what Peter lacked—the introjection of his mother's containing function. If this does not happen, Bick said, "the concept of a space within the self cannot arise" (p. 187). With no space inside, Peter felt unable to allow space between us outside, and only very gradually allowed himself an idea of me as a separate person with a life and a mind of my own. He could not tolerate a silence in our sessions and, if there was what I might have called a pause, he experienced it as tormenting and persecuting. I did have the space to think—but only just. Balint thought of silence as having two possible meanings: "One is a frightening experience of a horrible emptiness, full of suspicion, hostility, rejection and aggressiveness, a silence which blocks progress and is on the whole barren" (1955, p. 239). I thought that silence, for Peter, would almost certainly bear these qualities.

It is also important to note that, whereas I have cited Susan's, Jean's, and John's aggressiveness as a factor in their progress, Peter was virtually unable to be really aggressive towards me: angry sometimes, certainly, but not really aggressive. Perhaps it was the fear of his aggression manifesting itself in the silence that largely stopped his allowing this to exist within our relationship. I imagine that Peter experienced the "overwhelming rage and distress" referred to by Tustin even more acutely than my other three patients, and it has, therefore, been very much harder to find a way of setting it free.

Initially, John also could barely tolerate silences, and it became apparent that, as he felt increasingly safe with me and more able to trust, there were more and more silences. These were mostly similar to the second type of silence described by Balint: "a tranquil, quiet experience of harmony, an atmosphere of confidence, acceptance, peace; a period of tranquil growth, of integration" (1955, p. 239).

Balint goes on to state that quite often the patient's silence is a mixture of the two antithetical attitudes. I tried to show earlier that this was what I experienced with Jean. Sabbadini (1991), too, in his paper, "Listening to silence", describes how it can be "a barrier . . . a shield . . . a bridge. It can be a way of avoiding saying something and it can be a way of saying what no words could ever tell" (p. 409). He says,

> Perhaps one of the main functions of silence is to transform unconscious anxiety, concerning some as yet unknown or unworked-through inner conflict, into more manageable, though often more painful, conscious anxiety specifically connected to the analytical relationship. [*ibid.*]

When there is a silence between us, the patient is communicating that there is something he or she is not able or not wishing to communicate. (For further discussion of "silence", see Chapter Eight, on "Absence".) The silence of Balint's second type is often experienced within an atmosphere of "potential space". Ideas are being thought about which will inevitably lead to some form of creativity and growth. There is a connection between patient and therapist and the atmosphere is something of a "friendly expanse"—a philobatic atmosphere.

The first type of silence described by Balint is experienced in an ocnophilic atmosphere. For instance, in a silence Peter feels persecuted by me, rejected by me, aggressive towards me. He is experiencing a "horrid empty space" and is desperate to return to a situation where he can pretend to himself that I am an object that holds him, although in reality I am an object that he clings to, desperately seeking safety.

Conclusion

I hope I have shown that the type of space created by patients in my consulting room will be a repetition of the way they have experienced the spaces in their infantile relationships.

Jean's mother was unavailable, so, as a small child, Jean found a friendly environment with animals, flowers, and books as a substitute for intimacy with people. In the consulting room, she found for herself an environment containing a couch, flowers, and pictures. Sheila's mother became unavailable, though Sheila may have felt at one time "fused" with her, and so she had been continually seeking fusion throughout her life in relationships where she could be "in love". However, because of her passionate relationship in the external world, she became more fused with my words and the setting than with me personally. John's mother was unavailable. Initially, he created a suspicious space between us and clung to the concreteness of the set time and pattern of our meetings. Only gradually could he trust the analytic space and allow the flow of togetherness/separateness from where potential space arose. Peter's mother was unavailable and often impinging. He clung to her as he later clung to me, desperately looking for holding and containment, utterly afraid of horrid empty spaces.

John and Jean found me dangerous; they turned to philobatism and the acquisition of skills for safety. However, these manoeuvres against intimacy and closeness were not really effective. Both patients admitted later that they longed for states of togetherness.

Sheila and Peter resorted to ocnophilia in an endeavour to make me safe. Finding objects to cling to in order to avoid the pain of separation and individuality seemed to be their way of denial of the separate existence of the other and the isolation of the self.

My efforts with each patient were to achieve a "harmonious interpenetrating mix-up" through our words and our silences, from which a creative separation and individuation could emerge.

Sometimes, however, I represented a dangerous first object (mother) who, through lack of constancy and reliability, posed a threat of annihilation to the developing infant. The infant/patient sought either ambivalently clinging relationships or a wish to master skills including those of relating, only in order to return to a safe distance—a friendly environment devoid of threatening objects.

When Winnicott discovered Darwin's *Origin of Species*, he wrote "the main thing was that it showed that living things could be examined scientifically with the corollary that gaps in knowledge and understanding need not scare me" (Phillips, 1988, p. 1). Phillips says of Winnicott that he wished not to close gaps, but to find a way of examining them. They could be potential spaces for the imagination (*ibid.*). As we have seen, a potential space implies both togetherness and separation, the paradox out of which creative play can take place. (As Debussy said, "music is the space between the notes".)

A gap, therefore, can be a "space between", where there is room for the play of speculation and space for symbolization. A gap can also be experienced as frightening, persecutory, and negative. For example, when a child waits too long for his mother, he is plunged into the reality of the gap that, to him, feels like a great gulf, and the disturbance is too great for the creation of play, space, and symbolization. Winnicott says, in these instances, "there could be a blotting out, and that this blank could be the only fact and the only thing that was real" (1971, p. 26). This is what occurred for Jean in her early life and was re-experienced with me.

Our task in therapy, then, as I see it, is to recognize and examine the spaces, gaps, and gulfs between ourselves and our patients, and, thus, to attempt to understand what has created these sometimes defensive and frightened stances that occur between us. From there, it is hoped we can create a space where the patient can safely individuate, separate, and develop his or her intensely personal idiom.

> Let there be spaces in your togetherness
> And let the winds of the heavens dance between you
> (Gibran, 1926)

CHAPTER THREE

A sense of entitlement: vicissitudes of working with "special" patients

"He never wants anything but what's right and fair; only when you come to settle what's right and fair, it's everything that he wants and nothing that you want. And that's his idea of compromise"

(Hughes, 1857, Part ii, Chapter 2)

"Patients with problems of entitlement experience themselves as undernourished while the therapist experiences them as insatiable"

(Tenzer, 1987, p. 270)

These epigraphs illustrating "a sense of entitlement" are, I feel sure, recognizable to us all. Patients such as these consider themselves to be especially entitled, with special rights and privileges. Moses and Moses-Hrushovski (1990) suggest three categories in attitudes of entitlement: normal, excessive, and restricted. Normal is related to that which is reality-orientated: that is, correctly assessing that to which one is legitimately entitled. My focus in this chapter is not on the normal sense of entitlement but on the two polarized extremes: either excessive, with considerable narcissism and grandiosity, or restricted, which they say is often a reaction formation where the patient is found to function in a modest and self denying way (see also Jacobson, 1959). Not surprisingly, we find that these are two sides of the same coin and one masks the other. As Moses and Moses-Hrushovski state, "narcissistic overvaluation and grandiosity often are accompanied by a strong undervaluation, a strong sense of worthlessness or impotence" (1990, p. 69). Many American theorists have taken as their starting point Freud's paper, "Some character-types met with in psycho-analytic work" (1916d), where, in "The 'exceptions'", Freud refers to patients who express their sense of "deserving" or of having suffered. These patients consider themselves special in the sense of being different from others. As Freud says, they feel they "have a right to be an exception, to disregard the scruples by which others let themselves be held back" (p. 315). Both "entitled" patients and those who are "exceptions" have the feeling that they have undergone particular forms of suffering in their lives and experience an enormous sense of privation or deprivation and injustice. These narcissistic injuries are variously enacted in our consulting rooms in terms of manic or hysterical type behaviour, envious and sadistic attacks, a controlling and withholding attitude in regard to fees and payment, and evidence of a reproachful attitude towards the therapist and the world at large. As a consequence, our countertransference is experienced either in masochistic feelings of self-blame for not being able to offer cure, or, on the other hand, variations on irritation, hatred, sadism, cruelty, and a wish to be rid of the patient. Feelings of revenge are very powerful, and can be a significant dynamic in the consulting room. In this chapter, through some clinical vignettes and an examination of the transference–countertransference dynamics, I shall be attempting to understand issues of technique that may be helpful in such cases, linking these with Rosenfeld's (1987) definitions of thick-skinned and thin-skinned narcissism. I shall also try to tease out any differences between the narcissistic feeling of being "an exception" and the ego attitude of entitlement, in an effort to understand whether this has implications for technique. Although this is an exploration of extremes, we need to be reminded here that narcissism is an important factor in healthy self-esteem, as is "a sense of entitlement", for ensuring that we get the rights that we deserve. This is all part of what Kohut (1966, in Morrison (1986)) refers to as the importance of "a healthy enjoyment of our own activities and successes" (p. 70) and the child's need to be "the gleam in the mother's eye" (p. 69).

Clinical example

This is from a case I supervised.

Alice (a woman in her thirties) presented for therapy after suffering from ME for some years. By all accounts, she had an intrusive mother and an unavailable father. From early on in the work, it became clear that she had a vulnerable and narcissistic personality and that she felt herself to be special and entitled. This took the form of needing a low fee and expecting that constant allowances would be made for her both by her therapist and, indeed, by society at large. When this did not happen, her sense of personal injury was profound.

The patient frequently adopted a sneering attitude towards her therapist and I understood this to be an omnipotent defence of Alice's to guard against fears that her therapist would ridicule her. Her envy of what others had was quite palpable (though denied by the patient), as was her aggression in sessions, and the countertransference experience was of rage and sadism. The therapist was often tempted to retaliate when caught up in an experience of being sadistically treated and emotionally manipulated. The patient's narrative usually contained elements of being short-changed, and in her outer life she was constantly fighting the Benefits Office to make sure she got her rights. No one could get it right for her: there was a fury with her parents, who saw her as sick, and a fury with the Benefits Office, who considered her well. Her therapist, too, had this profound sense that nothing she offered was of any use to this, apparently, grandiose patient, consumed with envy and a sense of injustice. It became clearer, as the work progressed, that Alice cheated herself of having her own experiences. She once made a revealing slip, saying, "part of me wants to be really ill" (having intended to say "really well"). Unless she is "ill", how can anyone know of the real illness: the sense of a defective mother having caused a defective self, or, in other words, a traumatic disruption in the patient's sense of perfection.

Over time, this patient could occasionally convey that she was terrified of being exposed or ridiculed, but mostly she clung to her contemptuous and superior attitude, inducing a sense of uselessness and stupidity in her therapist. There were ructions over an increase of fee, as she was "entitled" to a low fee, given her income and her illness. When Alice did not get that to which she believed she was entitled, there was a profound sense of hurt, rage, and betrayal, with a consequent wish for revenge. Nevertheless, from time to time, small insights denoted an inching forward and a dent in her defensive structures. For instance, she managed to suggest that her need to be ill was perhaps a need to be loved, and that she always felt that her parents wanted a boy rather than a girl.

Following a sense of advancement in the work (often revealed by her admission of vulnerability), this patient would move back into her familiar "retreat" of self-righteous complaints. She would become continually on her guard, wary of all her therapist's interventions as a plan to trick her into admitting something that would be felt as too exposing and/or humiliating. The therapist worked to show the patient how she both wanted and feared the therapist's analytic skills, as so often the therapist's interpretations were experienced as unbearably cruel, "using your theory against me".

The therapist frequently brought her sense of guilt and hopelessness to supervision, as well as her wish to shake the patient and bring her to her senses, and/or to retaliate, or, indeed, to be rid of her. Together, we tried to make sense of her feelings as countertransference, the outcome of the patient's projective identifications. I wondered with her about adopting a less interpretive approach; in other words, allowing the patient's grandiosity and tolerating Alice's enjoyment of feeling that it was she who was in control. This has some obvious benefits in terms of mirroring and positive attunement, but also pitfalls, as it could well feed the patient's fear of being totally destructive.

During this period, the patient had dreams of a psychopath—a plausible female killer who engaged people on her side and then killed them. The therapist interpreted the patient's dream as reflecting the patient's experience of her therapist as "luring her in for the kill", while at the same time knowing that this was something of her own experience with this patient. After considering the benefits of a non-interpretative stance, the therapist felt that her patient needed understanding through interpretation, as Alice's destructive and grandiose fantasies were gaining ground, as reflected in this dream of the psychopath, who is endowed with trickery and murder. I concluded that the therapist was right, as it was clear that her patient had become anxious about the dream and the subsequent rather paranoid experience of the therapist. I felt the accommodative approach would not contain the heightening anxieties, but that the interpretative response would address both transference and countertransference experiences, thus acting as a container for the patient's powerful projective identifications.

These two approaches towards the patient—the "accommodative" and the "interpretative" (Billow, 1999), also differentiated as the "gratifying" and the "frustrating" (Blechner, 1987)—are the basic dilemma for the therapist when working with patients such as these. I shall explore further thoughts regarding interpretative approaches later.

The therapy made small inroads for Alice through her wall of defences against shame, envy, greed, rage, destructiveness, and despair, but there was then panic and a reversal to projecting all this on to the other—mainly her therapist. Facing reality is facing the pain of being deprived, of not being perfect, of mourning, and, indeed, of the probability that she was never wholly loved for herself. It is a gargantuan therapeutic struggle to help the patient to give up this entrenched sense of "entitlement", which can be seen as reflective of an inner state of mind lacking the security and stability of a loving internal object.

My thoughts about contributory factors to this particular state of mind cluster around theories of narcissism, hysteria, shame, envy, and states of emptiness. I shall consider these, and cite other clinical vignettes in an effort to draw some threads together, which, I hope, may lead to further understanding.

Narcissism, "the exception", and a sense of entitlement

When Freud (1916d) wrote of the "exceptions", he concluded that these patients considered themselves such because they had some "experience or suffering to which they had been subjected in their earliest childhood, one in respect of which they knew themselves to be guiltless, and which they could look upon as an unjust disadvantage imposed upon them". Freud cites Richard III as an extreme example of someone who feels grievously wronged (because of his body shape), but he ends with the generalization that women claim privileges and exemptions due to their reproach against their mother for having "brought them into the world as women instead of as men" (p. 315)

So, in this paper, Freud is stressing suffering, disadvantage, difference, but also "Life owes me reparation for this, and I will see that I get it. I have a right to be an exception . . ." (p. 314). In other words suggestions of being entitled are here juxtaposed with the feelings of being an "exception". Later on, Freud suggests that Richard III feels "I may do wrong myself, since wrong has been done to me" (p. 315). Here, the notion of revenge is introduced. My understanding of Freud's ideas is that these personality types have suffered from a combination of external suffering and narcissistic vulnerability.

Rothstein (1977), writing on entitlement many years later, says that it is the *quality* of mothering (not suffering in itself) that leads to the attitude of entitlement, or the sense of being an exception. Not all handicapped persons see themselves as exceptions, he says (*ibid.*, p. 414). He states that persons fitting this description are narcissistic personalities who

> have experienced their mothers as confusing and contradictory—at one moment hostile, cold and rejecting, and at other moments overvaluing . . . The child clings to the memories of gratifying moments to form an attitude of "entitlement" in order to ward off frightening memories of mother's hostility or coldness. [quoted in Mollon, 1993, p. 92]

Patients such as these who come for analysis find difficulties in loving and in believing themselves to be lovable. (See Chapter Four for further exploration of these issues.)

These mothers have used their child to fulfil their own needs. The child's consequent feelings of entitlement enable him to deny the frustrating and contradictory aspects of his mother, protecting him from the sense that he cannot be loved for himself. A strong illusion has taken hold, defending against a deep sense of incompleteness and imperfection. "The gratifying moments when a child is being overvalued provide the experiences which serve as the anlage for the feeling of entitlement" (Rothstein, 1977, p. 409).

Steiner (1996), in a paper on revenge, seems to be thinking along the same lines as Rothstein in writing of patients who, in his terms, find themselves in a "psychic retreat" based on resentment and grievance:

> The sense of wrong experienced is made more painful if it follows a period of seduction by the primary object, who may have colluded in fostering the belief that oedipal intimacy is desired by the mother as well as the child. The result is that when this fantasy collapses the child feels that a promise has been broken, so that he is not only wronged but betrayed. [p. 435]

Steiner continues:

> The sense of right is easily transformed into an assumption of righteousness as the original split needs to be strengthened by projection of bad feelings, especially of guilt, into the third object. In this way the betrayal by the mother is denied and the belief is re-established that she will see the error of her ways and return to the idealised relationship. [*ibid.*]

Chapter Six addresses these issues of seduction and betrayal more fully.

Freud delineated his theory of narcissism in 1914(c), using the description, "His Majesty the Baby". The value of the development of this normal narcissism cannot be sufficiently stressed. Kohut (1966, in Morrison, 1986) quotes Freud's statement that "a man who has been the indisputable favorite of his mother keeps for life the feeling of a conqueror, that confidence of success that often induces real success" (p. 70). However, a person's consequent non-relinquishment of this "superior" (grandiose) position, clinging on unrealistically to *knowing* that he is a "conqueror", as opposed to *feeling* like one, may be seen as a central issue in difficulties of narcissism and entitlement. Conversely, an infant who never attains this position with his parents is defending against the terrible impoverishment thus caused. Freud (1916d) maintained that the claim to be an exception exists in us all, yet I am stressing in this chapter the excessive sense of entitlement from which the more narcissistically damaged individual does not recover in the course of "normal" development.

Would this indicate, then, that "a sense of entitlement" is relevant to all narcissistic personalities? I would venture to suggest that when narcissistic hurt and defence is prevalent, coupled with the feelings of having received insufficient love, that this is very probable.

At this point, I am making little distinction between being an "exception" (especially different) as a narcissistic way of living one's relationships and instances where one has adopted a "sense of entitlement" (i.e., of being especially entitled) to defend against the narcissistic illusion. All these types have restricted their capacity to live full emotional lives.

Defences employed to maintain "a sense of entitlement"

Defences of splitting and disavowal, as well as excessive use of projective identification, are used to guard against feelings of emptiness, envy, helpless rage, shame, love, and desire, and, thus, preserve the narcissistic illusion of perfection. These defences, then, are fuelled by resentment and grievance (Steiner, 1996) or grudge (Khan, 1975), based on a sense of having received insufficient care, recognition, and protection. Moses and Moses-Hrushovski (1990) and Mitchell (2000) also note the impact of the birth order and how a displaced child can feel cheated, deeply disappointed, especially deprived, and, therefore, entitled. Bell (1992), who suggested that "hysteria" could now be placed under the heading of severe narcissistic disorder, described the clinical presentation of patients thus: "there is an implicit demand from the patient that only their arrangement of things is acceptable" (p. 174). Britton (1999) concludes that the grandiosity in the hysteric is the illusion/belief that there is exclusive possession of the analyst's love. I believe this leads towards a tendency to hold the secret fantasy of being an "exception'. (Chapters Six and Seven also address issues that emerge with patients of the hysterical personality type.)

Kernberg (1975) writes of the establishment of a pathological grandiose self and a deterioration of internal objects as the basis of a profound and constant sense of emptiness. A grandiose self is one where we would find "a sense of entitlement" operating. This state of omnipotence (Rosenfeld, 1987) also defends against helpless rage.

"A sense of entitlement" operates as a powerful defence against envy, particularly where pre-Oedipal and Oedipal issues cannot be successfully negotiated. If I am entitled, then in my secret fantasy I am special, beloved, in control, possess all that is desired and there is nothing out there either to envy or to fear. The therapist faced with such a patient normally experiences in her countertransference the indignation and rage that the patient has needed to project or disavow. In states of emptiness and envy, entitlement is used to avoid mourning "the loss of the relationships one wishes one had had" (Bott Spillius, 1993).

In narcissistic states, we encounter defences against feelings of shame. In "entitled" patients, these are more difficult to identify. Mollon (1993) writes of a manic denial of shame, which he terms "countershame", and sees it associated with "paranoid ideation, constructed to rationalise the inner state, the unacknowledged shame" (p. 45). Patients' frequent and excessive use of projective identification in their relationships defends against awareness of these states.

Love and desire

Blechner (1987) poses the question, what is the inverse of entitlement? He tentatively suggests it could be "altruism". However, he subsequently concludes that all this does is reverse the object of entitlement, so that "I deserve" becomes "you deserve" and the quality of entitlement may remain unchanged. He then states that the

> essential inverse of the attitude of entitlement is in desire. The essence of entitlement . . . avoids the experience of the self-wanting, or needing, or desiring, and of the other as free to respond in a gratifying or frustrating manner . . . [It] avoids the immediate experience of interpersonal desire. [p. 245]

Blechner illustrates beautifully how the manifest attitude of entitlement often masks its true aim or object and gives an example suggesting a trial gratification. His patient was paying a reduced fee
and was fighting vociferously over a suggested increase. Eventually, Blechner suggested the patient pay what he felt right. After
an initially incredulous response by the patient, he paid the
analyst's full fee (i.e., more than the suggested increase) at the end
of the month.

The paradox here was that the patient *seemed* to be struggling
over the fee to which he felt entitled, but, while his claims *seemed* to
be overtly financial, his underlying desire was for something quite
different. Money was, in fact, irrelevant, but was the only way his
parents had expressed their love.

My understanding is that the discovery that his patient was
allowed to reach was facilitated by an attitude of love by the
analyst; albeit, this was clouded by his feelings of confusion, rage,
and degradation. He was still able to perceive and respond to something of the subjectivity of his patient when he told the patient to
pay what he wanted. The patient's final response—to pay a full
fee—may have been an identification with a parent who showed his
love through a gift of money, but, nevertheless, something loving
emerged in him, too. Thus, small increments are made in the analyses of such patients.

*Further clinical examples: countertransference reactions
to patients with attitudes of entitlement*

Barbara (a young woman in her twenties), another patient whom I
supervised, sought therapeutic help to support her, although it felt
more like "take her side", while she and her husband were going
through a divorce. Her history suggested that she was the only
child of a narcissistic mother and an unavailable father. She was
also still mourning the death of her father some months prior to the
referral. She carried the absolute conviction that she was in the
right, and that her view of things was correct and must be held by
her therapist. She conveyed that she was impoverished, that her
husband and therapist would deplete her, and that she was very
special. Like other entitled patients, she expected a low fee and

made her therapist feel useless, raging, and denigrated. Her therapist learned that she could expect nothing from the sessions with Barbara: not regular attendance, not to be listened to, valued, have any interpretations reflected on, or to feel useful in any way. She was a thing, dehumanized, and frequently felt that she was only "a potty for the shit"! The therapist would either be raging and fighting to get in and be noticed, or switch off and wait for the session to end. Much of the content of the sessions focused on money—how much she had, the large sum she could expect from the divorce settlement, to which she felt fully entitled. It was naturally all the more galling for the therapist, who was paid a minuscule fee.

On one occasion, the therapist confronted Barbara, proposing an increase of her fee.

The patient denied that she had money, saying it was her mother's. This was a session where every intervention by the therapist prior to the confrontation over money was answered by the patient in terms of "that's what my mother said", "my mother asked that", etc.

I think this was the patient's way of telling her therapist that mother had all the goodies and neither the patient nor the therapist had any. The therapist had also been in touch with a sense of emptiness in the patient and within the atmosphere of the sessions.

Both Alice and Barbara evoke similar countertransference reactions in their therapists—despair, hopelessness, rage, frustration, and a wish to retaliate.

By way of contrast, Emma (in her thirties), a patient of mine on a very low fee, often displayed a conscious attitude of restricted entitlement. She felt different, saw herself as a failure, born to suffer, undeserving, and, when she became ill, felt that was what she had deserved because her life was perceived as a failure. She would not let herself get a successful job or have a nice home, and even a cup of coffee at a restaurant had to be felt to be "deserved" before she would allow it. My understanding was that she held herself depleted, incapable, and unsuccessful as a constant punishment (revenge) towards her parents for giving such insufficient supplies of love and affirmation. This shallow defence became transparent when she could express her rage with her parents for allowing her to suffer as she did. It was verbalized in financial terms. They did not give her enough money, so how could they expect her to exist on the allowances they gave? Everyone knew she had been trying so hard to earn proper money, it wasn't her fault if she could not succeed, and now she was worn out with trying and it had made her ill. Thus, in the therapy, she oscillated between restricted and excessive entitlement. In either mode she felt impoverished, and in our sessions there was never enough time for her: she was different from other patients, she could not manage with fifty minutes—it simply did not suit her.

I believe it was because of the oscillation between the two modes that I did not feel totally raging and frustrated, as did the therapists of Alice and Barbara. This patient could carry some of these feelings herself. Sometimes, I felt hopeless, defeated, that I was the one who was the failure. Frequently, my interpretations were denied or reacted to with confusion or bewilderment—or even forgetting. "What did you say just now?"

I think an important distinction between Emma and the other two patients was that Emma came to own her real needs—love and recognition from her parents—and also to grieve for what she had not received. She began to understand over the first year of her therapy that money was the currency through which she was seeking what she really wanted (Blechner's earlier example). Because she was willing to admit something of her real wishes, she then became a patient who felt more loveable and her claims for, and attitudes of, entitlement became more modified. In my counter-transference, I began to be aware of loving moments, feelings which I have noted elsewhere (see Chapter Four) to be essential for the successful outcome of psychoanalytic work. As yet, neither Alice's nor Barbara's therapists can love them—they can barely tolerate them!

However, I also think that in this more loving mode, I turned a blind eye to the sado-masochism that underlay our relationship. I continued to receive a very frugal fee (a parallel with Emma's managing on insufficient rations), and, two years after we began therapy, she died, after suffering for some months from the return of a malignant illness.

In her own words, she came to therapy to "get a life", and she finished it with a death.

In what was to become our final session, she came to tell me that she had been given two months to live. She told me that she needed to know whether or not I had a supervisor. On exploration, this was about the fact that she knew that I cared for her and she was concerned about how I would cope with her death. There was certainly some real concern here, and during the session I was very moved. I never saw her again, although we spoke once or twice briefly on the telephone. She died ten days later. After this, I was more in touch with the other side of things—the sadism that was also present in this encounter.

I was left with a high degree of masochistic self-blame that has taken a good deal of working through.

Cruelty

The therapists of Alice and Barbara frequently resisted making an interpretation because they sensed it would be hurtful, cruel, and retaliatory, reflecting their current countertransference feelings. Both these patients induced this sense of cruelty in their therapists and it needed tactful and painstaking effort to tolerate this in the countertransference and eventually work towards relocating it in their patients. Brenman (1985a) stated that the source of cruelty is "the obliteration of the concept of the whole human mother that narrows the picture of the world to a cruel loveless place" (p. 278), which supports my thoughts about the inner world of these patients.

It is important to be aware constantly of the sado-masochistic elements in working with patients who have an excessive sense of entitlement. For instance, in the patient's mind, she/he is either suffering terribly at the hands of the sadistic therapist or she/he is triumphantly in control. The therapist, too, may be torturing herself in feeling denigrated, hopeless, useless, and unable to formulate an interpretation to the patient, feeling it to be cruel or untimely.

Main (1957) found, in a study of countertransference reactions of hospital staff to their "special" in-patients, that they became overwhelmed with a sense of failure and self-blame.

As the patients became increasingly insatiable, self-blame increased. Sometimes, the therapist was left feeling that nobody else but he or she could help this patient (i.e., that the therapist, too, was special). Main described the patients as tormented by childlike needs and rages, and, in turn, tormenting others as a defence against the dependence of primitive love. These patients' lives were beset with traumatic rejections, resulting in their behaving ruthlessly, sadistically, and with total disregard for their object. Had he written his paper some years later, he could have said these were patients with an excessive "sense of entitlement".

Main stressed the need for the sincerity of the therapists as an essential ingredient of the treatment. This involves an honest admission of the sadism and wish for retaliation that these patients induce.

Working as a supervisor, as I have been with the therapists of Alice and Barbara, there is the potential to be very helpful in this area, involving the need to process my own capacities for cruelty and sado-masochism.

Considerations for technique

As described earlier, many authors have advocated flexibility of technique. This is variably referred to as: the accommodative/interpretative (Billow, 1999); the gratifying and the frustrating (Blechner, 1987); restoration of harmony through recognition *vs.* confrontational (Grey, 1987); and mirroring and unmasking (Bromberg, 1983). These are different terms for essentially similar ways of working. Wright (1991) would have called them maternal and paternal ways of functioning.

Kohut is, of course, prominent among psychoanalytic theorists for advocating that the patient's grandiosity should have full expression. Other object relations analysts, such as Balint and Winnicott, would be somewhat in agreement with Kohut, in viewing attitudes of entitlement as expressions of need. I imagine that they would have considered the possibility of adapting to fit the patient, while, at the same time, they would have been formulating certain interpretations regarding their patients' demands for specialness. In other words, they would largely, though not solely, advocate the accommodative, gratifying approach. Tenzer (1987) writes of the necessity for a working alliance ("a bedrock of understanding", p. 268) to be established before the patient's illusions can be confronted.

I have found Rosenfeld's (1987) thinking about thin- and thick-skinned narcissistic patients to be very helpful in this area. He refers to thin-skinned narcissistic patients as having been repeatedly severely traumatized as children in their feelings of self-regard. They have managed to overcome and hide these feelings (vulnerability and shame) through maturation, and, indeed, they frequently adopt a position of superiority as compensation. This results in "the patient's sense of triumph and revenge against the parents or siblings" (p. 275). Rosenfeld warns against the analyst over-emphasizing their destructiveness, and stresses the need to help them to retain the positive aspects in their narcissistic organization.

Thick-skinned narcissistic patients, on the other hand, have "to be treated in analysis very firmly and have to be confronted with their narcissistic attitude and their envy. . . . With these patients the frequent repetition of interpretation and confrontation seems to be unavoidable" (p. 274).

Here, we have an indication of when to be thinking about which of the two approaches would be relevant at any one time to these "entitled" patients.

Britton (1998) has elaborated further on Rosenfeld's concepts, emphasizing the interchangeability in any one patient of these two qualities. He sees the essential factor in these two states as the result of two different relationships of the subject with the third object, within the internal Oedipus situation. The thin-skinned narcissist avoids the objectivity of the third object and clings to subjectivity. The thick-skinned narcissist identifies with the third object and renounces subjectivity. For the thin-skinned narcissist, the receptive/maternal transference is of paramount importance, while for the thick-skinned narcissist, it is the analyst's objective interpretation that is sought. As Britton says, "enlightenment seems possible but directly experienced desire or antipathy is not" (p. 51).

Bateman (1998), too, develops his thoughts from Rosenfeld's work. He refers to thick-skinned patients as "object-destroying" and to thin-skinned patients as "object-denying" (p. 14). There are moments when our largely thin-skinned "exceptional" and "entitled" patients can tolerate objectivity and the insertion of an interpretation (paternal mode), but these have to be carefully monitored. These patients do, in fact, often appear to us in their thick-skinned mode, demonstrating "impenetrable superiority" (*ibid.*, p. 15).

Bateman (1998) concluded that interpretation with thin- and thick-skinned narcissistic patients becomes therapeutically effective when a patient is moving between these two positions (p. 23), having demonstrated this with a detailed clinical example. "Only then is the patient's mind capable of understanding the thinking within the analyst's mind as formulated in an interpretation" (*ibid.*).

Steiner (1996) considers technique with patients who have buried their revenge. He states that if a patient can be encouraged to verbalize his hatred and wish for revenge, he could subsequently recognize these attacks as being subjectively owned and may lead to contact with regret and a wish for reparation. "If the attacks can be tolerated and properly analysed rather than condemned, resentment can give way to remorse and a move towards reparation can begin. Often this takes the form of forgiveness" (p. 438). It would seem that Steiner is here suggesting the usefulness of working initially with the thin-skinned aspects of his patient and then, having sufficiently tolerated these, there could be some space for the more thick-skinned, objectivity-seeking part of the patient to engage with the analyst.

Conclusion: entitlements and exceptions

These patients share a sense of having suffered terribly and wanting/expecting special privileges because of this. Both may display a sense of grandiosity in their relating, although it is more covert in those with "restricted entitlement". There is a blurring, as I have shown, between the "exceptions" (who feel different from other people and consider that ordinary rules do not apply), and those with the ego attitude of "a sense of entitlement" (who feel they have special rights). The wish for *revenge* is present in both, to a greater or lesser extent, and it would seem that the depth of the sense of *betrayal* would also determine the strength of the unexpressed revenge. (Again, see Chapter Six, on seduction and betrayal).

One distinction that I would like to suggest is that the "exceptions" as Freud describes them, suffer from *privation* (never having had), as opposed to those with "a sense of entitlement" who suffer from *deprivation* (having had, but then lost). I have reached this hypothesis through my understanding of the "exception" as someone who feels that he or she was born deeply wrong or deficient. These "exceptions" would, I suggest, be suffering from *privation*. In contrast, Rothstein's conclusions concerning "a sense of entitlement" derive from the notion of an infant that clung to the gratifying experiences with a mother. In other words, these infants have had, but then lost, their status as "His Majesty the Baby" (Freud, 1914c), and, thus, are suffering from *deprivation*.

Another useful differentiation would be to consider the "exception" as preoccupied with a defective sense of self, and "entitled" individuals as more preoccupied with their defective and disappointing objects. I believe that what I have described above would bear this out.

In privation, in the words of T. S. Eliot (1935a) in "Little Gidding", the analytic work will be to "know the place for the first time". Baker (1993) would see this as "The patient's discovery of the psychoanalyst as a new object'. When considering deprivation *vs.* privation, the therapist will need to bear in mind the kind of grieving that needs to take place. In other words, mourning the loss of an illusion (non-separation or "paradise") or mourning a deep lack from the beginning of life (no taste of "paradise").

Both these types of patients seek reparation and, when it is not forthcoming, grievance and resentment will turn to revenge. Alice and Barbara both felt impoverished and cruelly treated when their "rights" were not recognized—a repeated experience of a mother unable to offer the perfect "fit". Emma, although presenting with an attitude of "restricted entitlement", was locked into her psychic retreat of unconscious *revenge* (which, tragically, played a part in the destruction of her own life). She felt that she had been born different from all other members of her family and, thus, I came to think of her as typical of Freud's description of the "exception".

"The idealisation of death as the ultimate revenge is a theme familiar to analysts and involves a kind of unreality since the patient is both dead and also alive and enjoying the pleasure of revenge" (Steiner, 1996, p. 440).

Therefore, with regard to technique, it is important to assess the degree of unconscious revenge present in the patient. This revenge may be quite independent of whether it is attached to the more deep-rooted injury of the "exception" or the subsequent trauma of those with "a sense of entitlement". In addition, we need to be mindful of whether, at any one time, we have a thin-skinned or thick-skinned narcissistic patient in our consulting room and to be monitoring the movement between the two, which could guide us as to the appropriate mode of interpretation (maternal/paternal).

Grotstein's (1990) understanding of the complexities of working with patients with "a sense of entitlement" would seem a fitting place to end, stressing, as it does, the importance of this concept for our work.

> Entitlement stands at the boundaries of need, desire, self-assertion, self-expression, and aggression and is the veritable "glue" of ego identity and self-esteem. It represents a continuing legacy from what Winnicott has called the facilitating environment ("subject mother") and what I call the "Background Presence of Primary Identification," whose purpose it is to send its beloved ward off into the world of separation with a "blessing," the absence of which is experienced as a "curse" of nonentitlement ("bad karma"). [p. 62]

PART II
LOVE, HATE, AND THE EROTIC

CHAPTER FOUR

Love in the time of psychotherapy

"It is the physician's love that heals the patient"

(attributed to Ferenczi)

I t has long seemed to me that "love", in our work as psycho-analytical psychotherapists, seems to have been much neg-lected. I believe that most patients who present for analysis or psychotherapy feel themselves quite unlovable at some very deep level. My hypothesis in this chapter is that until and unless there can be felt moments of love for the patient by the therapist the patient is not able to develop fully. I think it is only when a patient can arouse our deepest loving feelings (not empathy) that we can really hope for a truly positive outcome from our work.

At times when I have questioned changes in patients, I have asked myself "Do I love X because he/she is making use of me and starting to change?" (my narcissism); or, indeed, "is it because I have found myself able to love him/her that growth and a sense of lovableness are now possible?" (allowing his/her healthy narcis-sism to develop). Paradoxically, I may discover my loving feelings when a patient is finally able to vent his/her rage and hate towards me or when a patient is struggling to reach, or has managed to reach, feelings of pain, loss, despair, joy, etc., either towards me or towards some significant other. I may find my loving feelings when a very "concrete" patient shows some capacity for play and symbolization. In other words, those moments, not of compassion, pity, or empathy, but of an unspoken rush of feeling of "I really love you" for a patient, can arise at various times and within many scenarios. In my first analysis, when I felt unlovable very often, even though I had many loving relationships in my life, I wanted urgently to know if my analyst loved me. Her wise response was something like "when you come to feel loved by me, then you will know". It was very true. It happened again in my second analysis. In hindsight, although many years of hard work and interpretation were undergone by both of us, what mattered most to me was that I reached a deeply felt sense of being lovable.

Theories on love

First, I shall endeavour to say what I mean by love, then to trace the various historical theories regarding love, and, finally, to give some clinical material for illustration. Coltart (1992b) speaks of love as a mystery, indefinable by the language of psychological theory. She also writes of qualities such as "patience, endurance, humour, kindness and courage", then adds "detachment" and states that they can "all be subsumed under the name of love. Loss or lack of it brings about depression, alienation, feelings of emptiness, and False-Self manifestations . . ." (pp. 118–119).

Suttie (1935) emphasized that the love bond comes from an emotion of tenderness ". . . more a mental sympathy than a genital relationship" (p. 31). It is this emotion of tenderness that I am referring to in this paper, although I would almost wish to call it "extreme" tenderness to distinguish it from a milder feeling. Suttie stressed the point that tender feelings and affection are not based on libido theory and sexual desire, but on the "pre-oedipal, emotional and fondling relationship with the mother and upon the instinctual need for companionship . . ." (p. 86). I believe my patients need to experience (or re-experience) the therapist as a loving mother. This would encompass Coltart's qualities listed above, although I feel that "detachment" is not present in more primitive loving states. To these qualities mentioned by Coltart, I would add containment and reverie (Bion) and the oft-missing ingredients referred to by Suttie: tenderness and affection.

I wish to emphasize, however, that these tender, loving feelings must emanate from one's most authentic self—there is no place for sentimentality in my ideas.

As I demonstrate, love is initially experienced through an "oceanic" feeling (Freud) or a "harmonious, interpenetrating mix-up" (Balint), but later matures into a separated out activity, with recognition of the other's subjectivity ("detachment"). Perhaps these earlier feelings are part of Coltart's "mystery"? In any case, I believe that more mature, object-related love is a derivative from the earlier oceanic feelings and primary love. I assume that both are present in my countertransference feelings, and are significantly linked to mother love. Unlike most mothers, however, I am unlikely to begin a new therapy "loving" a patient, though I may like him/her. Thus, I shall also be exploring what happens in the therapy to arouse my love, without which I am suggesting my patients cannot reach their capacity for loving and a sense of lovableness.

Moving now to history and Freud's statement in his *Three Essays on the Theory of Sexuality*, "a child sucking at his mother's breast has become the prototype of every relation of love" (Freud, 1905d, p. 221). Coltart called this first stage of Freud's theory on love, the "genetic". The second stage, she termed the "narcissistic", referring to his 1914(c) paper, *On Narcissism*, regarding the conditions for falling in love, and the third stage (the nucleus of object relations theory), "the expression of the *whole* sexual current of feeling; of the relation of the total ego to its object" (Coltart, 1992b, p. 114). By 1923, in *The Ego and the Id* (1923b), Freud had replaced the topographic model with the structural model, incorporating the ego ideal, and, thus, the importance of the object began to be emphasized further. In his 1930(a) paper, *Civilization and its Discontents*, Freud refers to "falling in love" and "oceanic feelings" (undifferentiated love), and, later, to "aim inhibited love" and "genital love" (differentiated love). The latter two imply more mature, object-related love and would, therefore, develop out of the former.

Since 1920, in *Beyond the Pleasure Principle* (1920g), Freud struggled with the antithesis between death and life instincts: the need to overcome hate with love. Later, Klein, too, was strongly influenced by Freud's ideas on libidinal and death instincts.

Likierman (1993) considers these ideas in her article, "Primitive object love in Melanie Klein's thinking". She has noted that most Kleinian papers, while emphasizing destructiveness and sadism, pay little attention to primitive loving feelings. Indeed, there is a current tendency to confuse loving feelings with a state of idealization, as opposed to an acceptance of an early object love arising "in response to the love and care of the mother" (Klein, 1937, p. 65).

Likierman identified two separate states in Kleinian thinking: that of "a normal primary experience of an ideal nature", and another where it is "defensively transfixed in a boundless, all-giving form" (1993, p. 251). She states that it would be quite erroneous to think that Klein believed the infant to experience only a defensive form of idealization. Ferenczi (1933) became convinced that it was necessary to separate early feelings of "tenderness" from a later, more mature, partly sexual love of passion, thus seeing love as having its own developmental phases (p. 166) from the beginnings of life. I feel my term of "extreme tenderness" to some extent combines the tenderness referred to by Ferenczi and Suttie with these feelings referred to by Klein and by Balint (primary love). I shall return later to ideas of the infant's love "in response to" the love and care of the mother.

Ferenczi's ideas, focusing on the role of the mother's loving feelings for the infant as vital for healthy growth, were a strong influence on Klein, and began to place an emphasis on the role of the mother that had, to a large extent, been overlooked by Freud.

Alice Balint's (1949) paper, "Love for the mother and mother-love", describes the archaic love that exists from the beginning in both child and mother. What the infant demands is absolute unselfishness from the mother—that she should "be there" or "not be there" as needed. "The ideal mother has no interests of her own" (p. 252) and the infant has a complete lack of reality sense in regard to the interests of its love object. This fundamental archaic love implies a mental state where there is a "complete harmony of interests" (p. 254).

She then goes on to examine the mother's archaic love for her infant, and sees in it the same lack of reality sense because "one's child is indeed not the external world" (p. 255). For the child, the mother is an object of gratification, and so is the child for the mother who looks upon her child as a part of herself. She calls this early relationship "instinctive maternity" as opposed to later "civilized maternity" (p. 256). She goes on to say, "The real capacity for loving in the social sense . . . (tact, insight, consideration, sympathy, gratitude, tenderness) . . . is a secondary formation" governed by the reality principle. She stresses the essential difference between maternal love and love for the mother in that "the mother is unique and irreplaceable, the child can be replaced by another. We experience the repetition of this conflict in every transference neurosis" (p. 257). So, in this archaic love, there is no reality sense toward the love object but "what we are wont to call love" develops directly under the influence of reality (p. 259).

Alice Balint has written about a patient who had within her "the deep conviction that it belongs to the duties of a loving mother to let herself be killed for the well-being of her children", and quotes a warm feeling, something like: "How kind of you that you did die, how much I love you for that" (1949, p. 251). This is most reminiscent of Winnicott's statement in "The use of an object", where the subject says, "Hullo object! I destroyed you. I love you. You have value for me because of your survival of my destruction of you. While I am loving you I am all the time destroying you in (unconscious) fantasy" (Winnicott, 1971, p. 105). This, then, also leads on to the idea that archaic love demanding the life of the other is what has to pre-date civilized love, that occurring within the reality principle—within the real world of objects.

In contrast to this destructive, devouring, archaic love, Michael Balint (1968) takes a gentler approach to primitive love and puts forward his theory of "primary love" as a more apt and useful concept than "primary narcissism". He likens it to "an all embracing harmony with one's environment, to be able to love in peace" (p. 65). So, while Freud (1930a) saw this feeling of fusion ("oceanic feeling") as a pathological phenomenon, being a regression to an early state of narcissism and an inability to relate to objects in the real world, Balint saw it as an essential stage of early development. He also felt that regression to this state would occur in important moments in an analysis.

Balint stresses the point that aggressiveness and even violence "may be used and even enjoyed, well into the states immediately preceding the desired harmony, *but not during the state of harmony itself* (p. 65, my italics). Winnicott also says "aggression is part of the primitive expression of love" (1950, p. 205). In "Hate in the countertransference", he says, "if the patient seeks objective or justified hate, he must be able to reach it, else he cannot feel he can reach objective love" (1947, p. 199). He also tells us "that the mother hates the baby before the baby hates the mother, and before the baby can know his mother hates him" (p. 200). He goes on later to say that "the patient cannot see that the analyst's hate is often engendered by the very things the patient does in his crude way of loving" (p. 203). (This is explored further in Chapter Five.)

In writing of love, I am not ignoring hate, rage, violence, and destructiveness, but I want to place the emphasis on love for the purposes of this chapter. I take a position akin to that of Michael Balint: that sadism and hate are secondary "phenomena—consequences of inevitable frustrations" (see Chapter Five). This is, of course, a very different approach from that of Klein, who has focused on the innateness of sadism.

Balint feels the individual is born "in a state of intense relatedness to his environment" (1968, p. 67). The primary objects that prove to be gratifying are normally, first of all, one's mother; during certain stages of analysis or psychotherapy, the therapist or analyst also becomes this primary object.

> In this harmonious two-person relationship, only one partner may have wishes, interests and demands of his own . . . it is taken for granted that the other partner, the object or the friendly expanse, will automatically have the same wishes, interests and expectations. [p. 70]

This is like the "archaic love" that Alice Balint postulates, in the sense of the "harmony of interests".

I have pondered on whether Michael Balint is talking of dependency or love. But I think he sees this as the most primitive form of love: the harmonious environment is the all-embracing love object and the infant can, according to Klein, too, respond lovingly to this love and care. Because there is a relatedness, however primitive, Balint rejects the term "primary narcissism".

Fromm (1976) distinguishes between infantile love and mature love. Infantile love says, "I love because I am loved" and "I love you because I need you". Mature love says, "I am loved because I love" and "I need you because I love you". "I love because I am loved" is a responsive love (Klein), while "I love you because I need you" would seem to be more in line with Alice Balint's ideas on archaic love and the "harmony of interests". Fromm's statements regarding mature love imply a sense of self and other: an adult, separated-out state of being.

I return now to Freud, whose paper, "Observations on transference-love" (1915a), warns the analyst to resist any tendency towards countertransference feelings of love. Freud states that it is dangerous to let oneself have tender feelings for the patient and it is imperative not to give up the neutrality acquired by keeping the countertransference in check. He goes as far as to say, "the love-relationship in fact destroys the patient's susceptibility to influence from analytic treatment" (p. 166). It would seem, therefore, that Freud felt that tender love, a feeling of fusion, and erotic love on the part of the analyst were all equally threatening to a successful outcome from analytic work. These views did not modify over time.

Searles (1959a), in total contrast to Freud, wrote a most frank and illuminating paper on "Oedipal love in the countertransference" and, indeed, is of the opinion, which I share, that the analyst's work with the patient has to realize within the patient both "the capacity for feeling loved" (p. 289) and the recognition of one's capability for being able to achieve mature love. He says later that the "patient's self-esteem benefits greatly from his sensing that he (or she) is capable of arousing such responses in his analyst" (p. 291), and feels that the degree to which a patient is able to arouse these loving feelings in the analyst will affect the "depth of maturation which the patient achieves in the analysis" (ibid.).

It might seem, therefore, that what I am trying to convey was said most lucidly and movingly by Searles in this 1959 paper, where he talks about the analyst's countertransference to the patient as "a deeply beloved, and desired, figure" (p. 286). I am making a similar point to Searles's, except that throughout his paper, love is Oedipal and not pre-Oedipal. In addition, Searles is referring to the analyst as *responding to* the patient's love and longing, or to the analyst's narcissism when the patient gratifyingly improves, or else to the likeable adult the patient becomes in the termination phase of analysis. Other love responses are attributed to the analyst's unanalysed transference feelings carried over from his own past.

My point, therefore, is somewhat different, in that I am stating that for many patients (particularly those with schizoid and narcissistic personalities), the analyst's love will need to be aroused by the patient *before* the patient is able to discover his/her own capacities to love and feel lovable. This was Klein's point—the infant finding his/her loving feelings *in response to* the love and care of the mother. Hence, I believe we are trying to work towards our patients reaching a state of lovableness within, and a capacity to love (out of intimacy and gratitude) their analysts truly, rather than all kinds of feelings which could be misconstrued as love, such as idealization, worship, clinging, and defences against hate. Indeed, if this does not happen, then I believe that the state of being, here described by Klein (1937), remains unchanged: "an unconscious fear of being incapable of loving others sufficiently or truly, and particularly of not being able to master aggressive impulses towards others; they dread being a danger to the loved one" (p. 63).

Before leaving this theoretical section, I hope I have made it clear that I have been referring to two kinds of love: archaic and civilized, infantile and mature, primary and secondary. While Freud considered the first kind somewhat pathological, feeling that it was a regression and not object-related, others since have disagreed, seeing this primitive love as a vital state of being which is, at times, re-felt in life generally and in the consulting room. The capacity for secondary, civilized, mature love arises out of the more enmeshed and primitive, but the latter is always present. Indeed, we may not always be aware at the time how primitive or otherwise are our feelings of love for the patients or theirs for us. It is possible that if I were to ask myself "Why did I feel I loved my patient at that moment?", I would find it difficult to define whether it was because I felt a "harmony of interests" or whether I felt a more separate, realistic caring, sympathy, or tenderness toward the patient. (I would hope, if I do momentarily lose my reality sense, this would be promptly regained!) I believe the same happens for a patient. Whether he/she loves the therapist because of a sense of "absolute unselfishness" on the therapist's part, or whether there is a deeply felt gratitude towards an other for insight, concern, etc., might be difficult to identify.

Clinical examples

Michael (aged thirty-two) came into therapy able to verbalize that he wanted to feel loved, and thought that he could achieve this with me by giving me a "brilliant" time with him and his being my "best" patient. His two fears were of being found to be mad, and of the extent of his neediness, which I might see and hate. He was also struggling hard to control his sadistic feelings, felt, in particular, towards his mother, though later experienced also towards a younger sibling and towards his father, who reportedly told Michael that he was "shit" without him. Michael had come to believe this, and previous failed marriages and failed businesses seemed to prove to him that he was incapable of being successful on any front.

About one year into the therapy, he brought into the session the book *Love's Executioner*, and, on exploration, one reason he wanted me to read this was that in it the therapist talked about finding something to like in the patient. Later in the session, I was coughing, and he said that I might have accepted cough drops from him.

Thinking about possible meanings in this material, I saw that Michael was preoccupied with loving feelings in one way or another. The book title seemed highly significant—who will be the executioner of the feelings? If he could get me to love him, would he then attack/destroy this love (shadows of past relationships), or was he trying to find something to love in me, which he was finding difficult, particularly with an impending break and the risk of my rejection of his loving feelings. I certainly had a sense that he experienced rejected, hateful, and destructive feelings towards me, which may have led unconsciously to my coughing. I could not be allowed to know about them, however, because cough-drops were suggested by way of reparation. It could also be possible that he felt he was choking me with his material—both wanting yet fearing to do so. Perhaps he carried cough-drops through a fear that I would be choking him with my interpretations?

Shortly afterwards, in the session prior to the break, he told a story about Noddy and Big Ears:

Noddy wakes up happy, feeling "it's a lovely day and I'm going to see my friend Big Ears." On the way he comments to people what a lovely day it is and how he's off to see his friend. However, when he arrives, Big Ears opens the door and says, "Fuck off, Noddy."

From this, I understood that there was an inner configuration of a Big Ears person who is telling the other (who is trying to be loving and friendly) to fuck off, and a Noddy person who wants a loving, friendly relationship and does not see the aggression coming. Just who is who in this picture may change from time to time. There is certainly an issue of hurt rejection. I see these feelings of hurt, rage, and rejection as secondary feelings (as Balint describes)—a response to recent feelings of not being lovable and acceptable to me. In the earlier years, a constantly felt rejection and humiliation was the time boundary around the session. If he came early, he felt humiliated by waiting and being seen to be needy; whereas if he came late, not only did he miss out on his session time but his fury and sadism might be detected. If only, he felt, I had a waiting room, then somehow he would not be so exposed as to what he was feeling both internally with himself and also towards me.

Some while into the therapy, I started to feel loving towards Michael because, although his behaviour was often seductive and devious, there were also glimmerings of efforts to make contact with me and to work and to play. (See Chapter Six.) It became clearer that many of his internal objects were cruel, uncaring, demanding, and sadistic, yet not all. I heard about a father who scooped him into bed when he was scared in the night and a grandma who felt safe enough to run to. He desperately wanted me to believe him and to trust him and I found he began to work and play more creatively in the sessions, developing a genuine interest in his dreams, instead of bringing them along to please me. Alongside his increasingly felt need of me, he became more openly attacking with vociferous complaints about not affording the fees, his thought that I had discharged him a minute early, hating the time boundary, and a fantasy of leaving a pile of shit on my carpet. Then, perhaps, like he was with his dad, I would be "shit" without him too. I, as object, had to survive his destructive attacks, then I think I could be "used" and also seen as loving, accepting him for whom and what he was, not what he was trying to be to win me over.

I probably began to love him as I was gradually allowed to know him; not his collusive, seductive performance, but a him who hated me because he had come to need me. Much later, he was also able to value me, and protests about the fee ceased. As I discovered his real hate, rage, fear, neediness, playfulness, and willingness to struggle, rather than a pseudo copy of it, I became aware of loving him, and there were moments of a sense of harmony. (This feeling of mine is also cited in Chapter Six in regard to Alex.)

As he slowly realized his independence, first from his family and later from me, he found he could acknowledge and even value those times of dependence on me and others. He lessened an attachment to a girlfriend that had been sexually but not emotionally gratifying, and he worked through some hateful and rejecting feelings towards his young son, who lived abroad. During this time, he freely admitted how much he had need of me. As I became both less denigrated and less idealized and he discovered some trust and safety, he ceased to feel so antagonistic and destructive towards his mother and found a way to re-establish a friendly relationship with her, after cutting her out of his life for some years. His relationships and his work life began to be handled with greater maturity and he often reported an inner dialogue he had with me during the gaps. He had internalized my loving attitude towards him and was in turn behaving in a more loving, less destructive and aggressive manner in his external life. As this was happening, it brought about some fear that he might be with me forever. He wanted to fix an ending date: he thought six months, I thought another year. However, being able to hold an idea that he could, if he wished, leave in six months without incurring my retaliation enabled him to stay another year. In that year he achieved the significantly more mature relationships that I referred to. (In Chapter Six, I refer to these as "post-Oedipal".) At the end of therapy, he thanked me for "giving me my life" and said the therapy had "meant everything to me". Follow-up appointments showed that he was able to consolidate his capacity to love and his feelings of being lovable. He developed "the capacity to be alone" (Winnicott, 1958) and a sense of himself as lovable for who he is, not what he does (Fromm, 1976). Importantly, once he could feel more lovable for who he *was*, what he *did* in terms of business achievements and emotional relationships became significantly more successful.

Jean (whom I have written about in Chapter Two, "Spaces in between") came to therapy telling me about the Hans Andersen fairy tale of "The mermaid". She identified with this mermaid, who had given up her tongue to try to win love. Her tongue was the instrument that would have expressed her feelings, but to express her needs made her vulnerable, humiliated, and, in her mind, would almost certainly end in rejection. She defended herself by contempt and superiority. We could say she came to me with a warning: "If I ever find my tongue again, that would certainly mean that I should be unlovable". Indeed, Jean was so often harsh and attacking that she was difficult to love. Yet, when I saw her tears in relation to images of two people together in a symbiotic relationship (a harmonious, interpenetrating mix-up), thus revealing the full extent of her yearning, I did begin to love her. Her internal objects were disinterested and disconnected, and so mostly I was made to feel as she felt as a child, trying very hard to make contact with an other who seemed not to see me at all as the person I was. Her image of me changed gradually over time. Near the end of therapy, Jean's image of me changed again. This is described in Chapter Two in the vignette with the dagger, where she was finally able to look at me openly and say, "Hello Jackie Gerrard." As I said before, we were both moved by the telling of this, and I felt very loving towards her, with a sense that she knew and even if she could not yet reciprocate, she could at least allow it and risk a greater intimacy. At the end of our final session, she asked for a hug, which we had, and she left me with the words, "I love you, Jackie Gerrard." This mermaid had found her tongue.

Jenny was an only child of twenty-six, who has also found "connecting" extremely difficult. She had felt unconnected to her mother as a small child and had an absent father who was away for long periods at a time. With me, she was highly anxious, sometimes to the point of incoherence, and seemed almost unable to "take in" from me in any way, although occasionally something I had said that seemed to be ignored at the time would be brought back by her. I was not allowed to know, at least not in the moment, that I was of any use to her at all, which created something of a hopelessness and frustration in me.

She seemed to be the type of patient described in Giovacchini's paper, "Absolute and not quite absolute dependence", where "helplessness is central to their pathology" and they also show a fear of lack of consistency, "so that their environment is perfectly predictable" (Giovacchini, 1993, p. 242). This results in difficulties in exploration and "play" in the therapy.

This places the therapist in a precarious position. He cannot deal directly with the patient's often conscious assertions of helplessness, and yet he cannot abandon his patient to terror. Furthermore, he is incapable of becoming the rigid character that the patient demands, and that he believes he needs. [p. 243]

(In Chapter One, I describe the difficulties of working with patients such as Jenny.)

Giovacchini emphasizes that the therapist must accept the patient's helplessness and rigidity, but, at the same time, maintain a foothold in his own reality. If the patient can tolerate this split, then treatment can proceed.

With Jenny, I became the useless mother she felt she had, and I felt as helpless in dealing with her as she felt in her dealings with the world. She seemed similar to Giovacchini's patient, who has no particular wish to understand herself, but looks solely for nurture and support. When she felt she did not get this from me (which happened quite frequently), then I was no better than a waste of time and money. With Giovacchini's patient, it was the shift from absolute to "not quite absolute" demands within a holding environment that enabled some form of play: "a not quite is gradually transformed into a transitional space" (p. 251). He says that the patient can begin to play with the paradoxes contained in her rigid reality.

However, some patients are unable to find a "not quite" zone and, thus, never manage to play (see Chapter One). Giovacchini suggests that perhaps, in these cases, the safety of the analytic setting does not overcome the catastrophic terror that blocks the ability to play. I do not yet know whether or not Jenny will find this zone. Our work and my thinking about it, however, have enabled me to find a link between play and love. Mostly, I am not able to find within me the loving feelings that I am sure Jenny needs, nor can she give or accept love with me or with others. Thus, I find that my difficulty in loving her does not allow for any movement in her capacity to form loving relationships. She has spent a lifetime as a hidden self where genuine love and genuine hate are both risky.

Riviere's (1936) paper, "A contribution to the analysis of the negative therapeutic reaction", mentions the horrors within the internal world: "the undying persecutors who can never be exterminated—the ghosts" (p. 144). Jenny resists becoming aware of what is within, insisting instead that she needs care, advice, and support. "Belief in better things is so weak; despair is so near", says Riviere (p. 146). There is barely a grain of hope, and yet the patient clings to analysis as there is nothing else.

My struggle with Jenny is ongoing. I certainly do feel that I need to find an entrée into my loving feelings for her before she can safely dare to reach for her own. My difficulties centre around the problems in locating her true feelings and in establishing a "not quite" zone where play could take place and with it a space for love and hate.

Conclusion

We have all moved a long way from Freud's ideas of 1915 that analysis should be carried out in the state of abstinence or privation. However, it is still difficult, I think, for the analysts and psychotherapists of today to think about tender feelings towards their patients. For instance, Kernberg's book, *Love Relations* (1995), refers only to the analyst's countertransference in terms of erotic responses, and writes of patients who experience

> erotic longings in connection with unrequited love . . . Patients with borderline personality organization may manifest particularly intense wishes to be loved, erotic demands with strong efforts to control the therapist, and even suicide threats as an effort to extract love by force from the therapist. [p. 115]

Balint (1968), however, could allow for his patient "to live with him in a sort of harmonious interpenetrating mix-up" (p. 136); in other words, offering the possibility of primary love. Searles allowed far more rein to his countertransference feelings and their vital importance, but he was, on the whole, referring to the developmental stage of Oedipal love (romantically and erotically involving the therapist), while I wish to state that (a) the love of the therapist for the patient can certainly be pre-Oedipal, and (b) more importantly still, that until and unless the therapist finds these loving feelings within him/herself, the patient will be prevented from making the developmental changes that need to occur in the psyche for the depressive position to be reached (Riviere). To my mind, genuineness, a wish for connectedness, and a capacity for work and play in the patient are the principal ingredients which will engender loving feelings in the therapist.

Finally, I hope I have not conveyed that love is all that is necessary in a psychotherapeutic relationship, because that is far from what I intend. Interpretation (and other agents for psychic change (Stewart 1990)) is vital to the work and to allow the patient to feel understood. Sometimes, however, especially for quite regressed patients or those with a very weak ego (M. Balint, 1968; J. Klein, 1990), interpretation is felt as unhelpful or even, at times, persecutory to the patient. Love is certainly not enough, but then again, in my view, neither is interpretation, containment, reverie, or any other psychoanalytical activity without the backing of love.

CHAPTER FIVE

Love and hate in the therapeutic encounter

"You stand at the blackboard, daddy,
In the picture I have of you,
A cleft in your chin instead of your foot
But no less a devil for that, no not
Any less the black man who
Bit my pretty red heart in two.
I was ten when they buried you.
At twenty I tried to die
And get back, back, back to you.
I thought even the bones would do"

(Plath, 1985)

"Psychoanalysis is in essence a cure through love"

(Letter from Freud to Carl Jung [1906],
as quoted in Bettelheim, 1983)

I n Chapter Four, "Love in the time of psychotherapy", I explored the importance of love in the therapeutic encounter, positing that for a successful outcome in therapy, a patient needed to engender loving feelings in the therapist. An assumption was that hate was part of the primitive, archaic feelings, but was not present in the feelings of mature or civilized love. At the time of writing, I omitted to take full account of the significance of the therapist's hate as a valid, indeed vital, ingredient of the capacity to love. It is clear that there is more to say about this than that "sadism and hate are secondary phenomena—consequences of inevitable frustrations" (see Chapter Four).

This chapter is an endeavour to bring hate into the arena of love in its totality.

I shall say what I mean by love and hate, review some of the literature on hate and its relationship to love, and then give some clinical vignettes which will demonstrate various situations where countertransference hate, if successfully overcome, can enable both transference and countertransference love to emerge. I shall also try to explore some of the similarities and differences between primary and secondary love and hate.

In Chapter Four, I defined love as "extreme tenderness" (Suttie, 1935) based in the pre-Oedipal, emotional, and fondling relationship with the mother. I also referred to the work of Coltart and Bion when taking full account of the concept of love, so I will not repeat that here.

The two kinds of love that I posited were "archaic and civilized, infantile and mature, primary and secondary", the first accompanied by enmeshment and (usually) ruthlessness, the second more separate and reality based. I concluded that certain patients could engender love through "genuineness, a wish for connectedness, and a capacity for work and play", and some clinical vignettes demonstrated how the presence or absence of the therapist's love affected the outcome of therapy.

By hate, I mean an intense dislike, a feeling of enmity and rejection, and a wish to hurt, or even destroy, the other. However, when thinking of primary and secondary states, my use of the word "hate" corresponds with my thinking on love. The primary state is where there is no clear delineation between love and hate, or between self and other, both involving an intense and ruthless relatedness to the (m)other.

The secondary hatred that I posit in this chapter has within it the wish to relate, so that, while the object is being attacked, hurt, destroyed, it is involved deeply and intensely with the subject. What differentiates it from primary aggression/hate (or ruthless love) is a greater awareness of separation of self and other (a relatively late stage of development) and the resulting intentionality of the wish to hurt. Thus, in my view, while I am hating you, I am wanting to have an effect on you: I need you to be involved with me and affected by me.

My use of the term primary hate could perhaps be more clearly defined by using Winnicott's "primary aggression". Winnicott, in fact, sees hate as a later development—the neonate does not feel hatred, he feels greed and ruthless love.

Winnicott helps to differentiate these early primary states that I am describing. Based on Freud's erotic and aggressive components, he links the aggressive with ruthlessness and the erotic with the "sensuous co-existence" of baby in an unintegrated state with mother (1950).

Primary aggression is seen to be hateful, cruel, and destructive, but only incidentally, that is, not intentionally. The infant is not yet separate enough from the mother to know of his ruthlessness. It is his aggression that allows for the Not-Me experiences to develop and is "only brought into being by active opposition, or (later) persecution" (Winnicott, 1950, p. 217).

It is in the sphere of the object relationship, and at a secondary stage of development, that I see anger as most clearly distinguishable from hate. I accept the *Oxford Dictionary* definition of anger as "extreme displeasure", which does not necessarily imply the wish or need for connectedness. When I feel angry with you, I may want you to know this or I may not. I may want to blot you out, or, again, I may not. My anger may lead to hatred, but is not, of itself, hatred. My anger separates me from you; my hatred and my love connect us.

I have been helped with this formulation by Bollas (1987a), who takes issue with Freud's original thinking, whereby hate is allied with the death instinct and love is placed among the life instincts. Bollas offers us the term "loving hate"—"a situation where an individual preserves a relationship by sustaining a passionate negative cathexis of it" (p. 118).

Bollas places a valuable emphasis on the preservation of a relationship that can only be felt to exist where love would seem to be unavailable. This is particularly notable in schizoid personalities, where love is considered dangerous.

Winnicott (1947) writes of the hate of mother for baby and of analyst for patient, and stresses the importance of finding a way to acknowledge this with a patient prior to the ending of an analysis. This is in the area of secondary hate. In a later paper, Winnicott (1950) states clearly that he sees aggression as "part of the primitive expression of love" (p. 205), and writes of infants in the state of pre-concern, where ruthlessness includes attacks on the mother's body: these are felt to be acts of love. (Primary aggression=ruthless love.)

I described, in the previous chapter, Alice Balint's (1949) concept of archaic love. Alice Balint and Winnicott would seem to be in agreement that this type of archaic or ruthless love, which has an excessively ruthless basis, contains destruction in fantasy. Thus, Winnicott's statement, "While I am loving you I am all the time destroying you in (unconscious) fantasy" (1971, p. 105).

In this area, too, Freud, in *Totem and Taboo* (1912–1913) wrote about ruthless relationships, for example, those obtaining between sons and their "violent primal father" (p. 141). Loewald (1979) took up this theme of "parricide", and stressed the necessity of it in symbolic form for a successful negotiation of the Oedipus complex.

I wish to stress that these primitive fantasies are necessary to healthy development, in order for normal growth into later relationships with their differentiated emotions of love and hate. This is beautifully described by Winnicott in "The use of an object" (1971).

Norrington, in her unpublished paper "Hate in the counter-transference" (1996), claims, in agreement with Winnicott, that "it is only through the recognition of intensely felt hate, that we can come to love and feel concern for the object who has survived our hate through his own resources rather than being magically restored through omnipotence".

Norrington has differentiated anger from hate: anger as connecting and binding, and hate as separating. It is in this area that I have found it helpful to think about primary and secondary states of being. In a primary state (pre-ruth), ruthless attacks on the mother's body—hardly differentiated from the infant's own self and body—involve a "mix-up" of love and hate, alternating states indiscernibly separate from each other. Vital to both these experiences of love and hate is an intense primitive relatedness to the other.

In a more differentiated state, hate and love are more separately felt and experienced. It is here that I would be in agreement with Bollas, as opposed to Norrington, in terms of hate serving as a means of connecting, while I would see anger as separating. In this secondary form of relationship, hate is much more clearly discernible from love, but, nevertheless, is also felt as part of an intense relatedness. It is often said that the opposite of love is indifference, rather than hate. My stance is that while I am hating you, I am all the time relating to you. When I am angry with you, I want to cut you off and blot you out.

It is this secondary state of hate that Winnicott (1947) refers to when discussing objective or justified hate, which has to be reached before patient (and analyst) can reach objective love.

Like Bollas, Gottlieb (1994) stresses that hate contains "the wish to know, and be known by, another" (p. 18). She makes an important distinction between "objective" hatred and hatred resulting from the projection into the therapist of a hating internal object. This may be a distinction that is important to make, but, when in the presence of an attacking, contemptuous, destructive, borderline patient, it can be a Herculean task to do so.

If love and hate can be recognized and experienced separately (as opposed to the "mix-up" in primitive states), the "loving hate" of which Bollas writes can eventually give rise to a freedom, without danger, for the expression of love in a less repressed form.

"Hate emerges not as a result of the destruction of internal objects, but as a defence against emptiness. Indeed, it represents an effort to emerge from this vacuum into object relating" (Bollas, 1987a, p. 130). Hence, hate, either in its primary or secondary form, (Bollas is describing the latter), with its associated striving to relate, may often be a forerunner to love.

Gabbard (1991) concluded that the goal of termination is not to eradicate hate, but to temper it with love, having introduced us to his paper with a quotation from Samuel Butler: "It does not matter much what a man hates as long as he hates something".

In discussing technique, Carpy (1989) and Slochower (1991) have both advocated allowing elements of the countertransference hate to emerge in a modified way with the patient, Carpy through what he calls "partial acting out", and Slochower through "the extremely firm, absolutely non-intrusive, and sometimes *mildly annoyed* analytic stance" (p. 713, my italics). In other words, both analysts believe in the importance of letting patients know they have made an *impact*, which conveys a living relationship, but one where the hate is survivable by the analyst. Coltart, too, in her papers "What does it mean: 'Love is not enough'?" (1992b) and "Slouching towards Bethlehem" (1986), stresses the importance to the analytic work of letting patients know the impact they have on the therapist. In both papers, the analyst's expression of hatred conveyed the depth of the feelings towards the patient, and the expression of intense hatred paved the way for the loving relationship to develop—one where the capacity for work and play was restored.

Prodgers (1991) endeavoured to "lift the lid off some of the shame that still abounds in respect of our hate in the countertransference" (p. 153) He suggested that, for many therapists, there is a blind spot towards their hate which, if not uncovered, could cause an impasse in the work. These struggles, so relevant for me in my clinical work, are referred to in Chapter Six, on "Seduction and betrayal", and Chapter Eight, on "Absence", where I am working towards finding a space for love, work, and play.

Clinical vignettes

Paul

I saw Paul three times weekly, and was warned early on of the likely sabotage of his therapy. He introduced me to what he called "the enemy within", which was part of an internalized, parental, scornful, and contemptuous object. Month after month, he attacked his therapy passively by an increased opting-out from life and work, and more actively by constantly saying that it was only a matter of time before he left and that nothing would change unless there was a magic wand.

Paul was a patient compulsively tied to his bad object (Armstrong-Perlman, 1991), and the hatred he could feel towards her was often projected into me as I began to feel like little Paul, tormented by a chronically hopeless, discontented, and persecutory mother-figure. In one session, overwhelmed by my own sense of impotence and hatred, I suggested to him that he seemed to need me to feel with him the hopelessness and hatred he felt as a young child, that nothing he could say or do would make an impact. (My inner experience was of being tortured and tormented.) This intervention led, for a while, to his renewed faith in me. When he felt more connected, he offered me a "gift": he told me that his partner felt he had changed significantly for the better at home. In my temporarily renewed sense of not being entirely useless and rubbished, I could refind some warm and loving feelings for Paul and, it would seem, he for me.

Slochower emphasizes the need, if the holding environment is to work with certain borderline patients, for the analyst to hold "their ruthlessness and rage and also analytic self blame" (p. 716). One might argue that, in my intervention, I had temporarily stopped holding these. That may be so. One might also argue, however, that it was necessary for us both to be reminded briefly that loving feelings could be experienced among all the hatred.

However, Paul was not to remain in therapy. He felt that I had damaged his protective disguise when some of his more affectionate and attached feelings had gradually emerged. He increased his antidepressant medication and returned to his life-strangling, self-destructive behaviour. This was underpinned by his belief that, if he mourned and separated from his dead internal object, he would have betrayed her. So, our analytic work was abandoned and, instead, he let me go and held on to the status quo. Sadly, therefore, Paul, a patient with whom I could find fluctuating feelings of both love and hate, left therapy before there was any true working-through of these deeply felt affects.

Stuart

Another patient, Stuart, sabotaged his therapy finally by not paying me, allowing his cheques to bounce. There had been prior warning of this several months earlier, when the first cheque bounced. I had been unable to make any real contact with this highly narcissistic young man, who kept me firmly at bay through his dilemma of should he marry Miss X or Miss Y. Each session, a new drama emerged, enraged with one of his women and drawn to the other, while I felt like a helpless bystander or member of an audience watching the players on his stage. As with Paul, I felt belittled and useless, as I know he, too, had often felt in childhood. He seemed to be desperate both to connect and to make sure he did not connect with me (the schizoid dilemma (Guntrip, 1977)). The unconscious way Stuart found to make contact with me was through various stories about his work with children. I found in him a deep empathy and compassion for children, and through this he aroused my love. But, in any personal way, connecting through love was too dangerous and would leave him too vulnerable, so he involved me through hate, excluding, obliterating, denigrating by non-payment. This ensured we remained in an intense relationship, apparently disconnected and yet, as I felt it in my countertransference, deeply connected. However, this was another patient who, although I could reach moments of love and tenderness as well as moments of hatred, sabotaged the therapy before he could work through his feelings and reach a degree of insight.

Christine

By contrast, my work with Christine was better able to illustrate the movement in the therapist between love and hate and the beginnings of a situation where countertransference feelings of love begin to emerge and can take firmer hold. Christine was a depressed, deeply schizoid patient apparently unable truly to love her significant objects—husband, children, and her therapist. The transference relationship she developed was of a distant polite co-operativeness, depressed and with little evidence of lively play and imagination, or, indeed, of much involvement or dependency. Separations seemed not to have been significant or to have an impact. (Christine was a patient who had experienced several traumatic deaths in her young adult life, and who, as a child, had spent an extended period away from her family in hospital.) Over time, however, it became increasingly noticeable that she cut off emotionally prior to a break. It seemed that the system had just shut down to deal with the circumstances.

As I noticed these barely perceptible responses to breaks, Christine gradually became increasingly negative towards me: sometimes through her complaints about the awful objects in my room, sometimes through her statements about what a waste of her time this therapy was—such a chore to come. I found that I became more drawn to her through thinking about her in between sessions, worrying about what I had said or might say in order to create more connection between us. I started to feel from time to time that I hated her, and was, thus, able to understand how her depression and isolation was her way of avoiding her hatred of the objects who had deserted her, either physically or emotionally. (See Chapter Eight, where my absent patient evoked similar feelings in me.) Christine was a patient who, in terms of love (Chapter Four), had not elicited my tender feelings or my capacity to offer her the opportunity to experience herself as lovable. In fact, she often presented, in the way Freud describes in "Mourning and melancholia" (1917e), a total and utter self loathing, the rage, hatred, and disappointment towards her objects having been turned back on to herself.

Later, Christine was able to recognize her own destructiveness and hatred. She expressed this with tears about the love she had withheld from a now dead parent. In that session, she was in touch with herself as a vengeful and withholding person and also with the despair that reparation could not be made because the parent had died. As she sobbed uncontrollably about this irretrievable situation, I discovered deeply tender and loving feelings towards her. She was unfreezing and, thus, owning her feelings. Subsequently, she began to talk of hatred, both towards her dead objects for dying, and towards her live objects for growing up and growing away from her, apparently rendering her useless and spurning her love. I was, therefore, beginning to understand that, certainly in part, the hatred I felt towards my patient was hers towards her objects for being ungrateful for the love she was bestowing upon them and also for deserting her. At these moments of understanding, my hatred dissolved and my love blossomed. Christine was owning her feelings and was showing courage in doing so. This allowed for some potential space, and I felt connected to her as she expressed her thoughts, fantasies, and memories. We had moved from a state of emptiness and occasional "loving hate" (in a desperate struggle to ward off the emptiness) and begun to reach an area where love could emerge.

Cathy

Cathy was a patient whom I saw for some years. She came for therapy because she was so filled with hatred towards her children that frequently she could not stop herself from physical violence towards them. Her early life had been deprived, both in terms of actual poverty and emotionally; she was one in a family of many children whose father had deserted, and the mother seemed not to have had the emotional capacity to relate to Cathy. Thus, she had no solidly good internal object. She was also handicapped by great envy, of her own children and of other women. This envy certainly extended to me, and there were frequent attacks on me and on the therapy, mostly in the form of "forgetting" to come to sessions, but also in covert remarks about my religion and my "stupid rules". There was a subtle blotting me out by a fixed conviction that, while therapy was a treatment that she needed, I as a person barely existed in her mind as someone to whom she might relate. There appeared to be a total lack of curiosity about me, and no acknowledgement that we had a relationship as two people who might matter for each other, or, indeed, miss each other at break times.

She attacked me in a much less florid way than some borderline patients. Nevertheless, for a while, I feared and dreaded our sessions, and actually became somewhat paranoid, anticipating attacks and concocting self-defensive arguments about why I had done or said such and such. However, over time, I must have done a good enough "holding" job, particularly in the area Slochower mentions, that of analytic self-blame, as slowly Cathy became more able to use the analytic space. She brought occasional dreams and wanted to understand much more of her own paranoid reactions in the world out there. I gradually became an important and helpful object to her, and as the hatred (in both of us) turned to love and gratitude (in both of us), Cathy made a most significant statement. She told me that her therapy with me had radically changed her attitude towards her children and allowed her to love them realistically, so that she felt she had been able to change the impoverishment and disturbance in the line of children in her family. As I became able to love her, with her increased ability to use me and the analytic space, she came to love herself and her children, the hatred of both slowly evaporating and giving way to the love. This, of course, does not mean that moments of hate were not still experienced in the relationship between us. When I raised the fee, she reacted with a flash of fury and a dismissive and denigratory comment, which gave rise to an equally furious response in me, and

I recalled one of Winnicott's reasons why the mother might hate the baby: "he is ruthless, treats her as scum, an unpaid servant, a slave" (1947, p. 201).

Janet

Finally, a therapist had a patient, Janet, whose mother had been somewhat idealized and had died just prior to the onset of therapy. The patient seemed unconsciously to have sought therapy to work through the hate she had always felt towards her mother. Janet felt that insecurity and disappointment had clouded their relationship. This had not been verbalized while her mother was alive. For a considerable time, the patient kept up a sustained attack on her therapist—she was contemptuous, dismissive, hostile, and very critical. The therapist managed an admirably receptive stance, able to consider carefully the origins of the patient's almost unrelenting attacks, and resist from any semblance of retaliation. From time to time, she would comment on her patient's hatred and the patient could join her, so that they could reflect together and some analytic work could be done. It was at moments when the patient could sob about the horrible person she really was, could feel true remorse for the perceived destructiveness she had invoked and the possible hurts she had caused, that the therapist could feel tender and loving towards her patient. At these moments, the ruthlessness had moved into a secondary stage.

Winnicott (1947) aptly described what happened here

> . . . in certain stages of certain analyses the analyst's hate is actually sought by the patient, and what is then needed is hate that is objective. If the patient seeks objective or justified hate he must be able to reach it, else he cannot feel he can reach objective love. [p. 199]

In these clinical vignettes, would the patients' reactions be seen as objective hatred or as a projection of the hatred into the mother/therapist? This is a real dilemma when trying to understand objective hatred and its distinction, as suggested by Gottlieb. Maybe both processes can occur at the same time. In the case of patients like Paul, Stuart, and, to a lesser extent, Cathy and Janet, dominated by internal hating and/or denigrating objects which led them to behave in a hateful way towards their therapist, the therapist's hating response to her patient may be something that is both "objective", because of the way she has been treated, and introjective, because of what has been projected into her.

The more helpful differentiation may be the one between primary and secondary states of hating. A primary state of hating is virtually indistinguishable from a primary state of loving. I hate you, therefore I love you is the same as I love you, therefore I hate you. It is in the area of primary process thinking. By contrast, a secondary state of hating is clearly separate from loving at the moment at which it is felt. When I hate Cathy, or when Christine rejects me or hates herself, love is not available in the transaction. It can exist beforehand, it can occur again within moments afterwards, but the two feelings are separate. Similarly, when Bollas gives us "loving hate", he is clear that it is the hate that unites the two subjects: for the ultimate purpose of love, certainly, but one feeling is clearly in the ascendant at the time of the experience.

Love is then incomplete without hate (and vice versa). They are bound up together in a kind of "mix-up" in primary states, or in the shadows in the case of secondary states.

The task for the therapist is to try to reach the love, but inevitably, at some point in the work, it has to be reached through the experiencing of hate, else it may be something other than love— liking, sentimentality, kindness, compassion, pity, etc. Patients must engender love in the therapist if they are to know that they are truly lovable. To have generated this love without the hatred having been rather intensely felt on both sides may be a hollow achievement.

How many times have we ourselves felt, and heard from our patients, "If they knew what I was *really* like, they wouldn't love me/employ me/associate with me". If I, a therapist, know that I have hated my patients, and if I also know that my therapist has hated me when I was a patient (how could she not, since I behaved disgracefully and hatefully towards her for this very purpose?), then any resulting love cannot but have more solid foundations and be trusted more readily to endure, to be real, to be true.

There is a fluidity of movement in psychoanalytic work, whereby love can rapidly turn to hate, then hate becomes resolved and love prevails. Sometimes, the more primary states obtain where all seems to be a "mix-up". So, the patient who can one day, or at any one time, feel remorse, love, and a readiness to work and reflect, can at other moments hate with intense passion. If all goes well, however, in time hate will be somewhat understood and overcome, though, one hopes, not dispensed with, and love will be more readily available. Our therapeutic aim must be for patients and their therapists to reach a point where they are free to love both themselves and one another.

CHAPTER SIX

Seduction and betrayal

"The trauma of oedipal seduction and betrayal may be a universal situation of danger"

(Josephs, 2006, p. 435)

T his epigraph sets the scene for this chapter, which addresses the universality of seduction and betrayal and its ubiquity in the analytic setting. My purpose is to explore how best to work with these "situations of danger" so that patients may be enabled to revisit their Oedipal issues fully within their analyses (Rusbridger, 2004). I suggest the existence of a *post-Oedipal* phase of development, where seduction, betrayal, and consequent revenge fantasies are no longer operative or dominant to the same extent. Finally, and perhaps more controversially, I suggest that moments of successful seduction, and, thereby, Oedipal triumph, may be an essential part of each and every analysis (Davies, 1998a,b).

Seduction and betrayal are issues that arouse "exquisite human vulnerability" (Josephs, 2006) in our most trusting and intimate relationships. A child, as the excluded other in the Oedipal triangle, may well have feelings of a resentful and humiliated loser, and, if

the experience of seduction and betrayal has proved to be traumatic, he/she may grow up to become an adult who will seduce
and betray others as they have betrayed him/her (Freud, 1910h).

This theme seems to arise continually in working with patients
generally, but particularly when working with those of a hysterical
personality type. According to Mitchell (2000): "In hysteria . . . it is
the seduction, not the consummation, that counts" (p. 144). She goes
on to emphasize the notion of a seduction taking place within a
three-person relationship, that is, the seducer, the one with whom
the seduction is enjoyed and shared (the seducee), and the one to
whom hostility and aggression are directed. I would suggest that, in
the consulting room, the "third" may be the imagined partner of the
seducer, seducee, or perhaps the analyst's psychoanalytic institu-
tion, with its "rules" of behaviour. In the UK, there is very little
reference in psychoanalytic writing to these issues of "seduction and
betrayal" manifesting in the consulting room, which has prompted
me to try to bring some thoughts together on my recent work. These
have been greatly stimulated by the work of various relational
psychoanalysts, in particular, Davies (1994, 1998a,b, 2003) as well as
Charles (1997), Davies and Frawley (1992), and Hoffman (1998).

It is true that, throughout the psychoanalytic literature, we will
find references to Freud's seduction theory and then to his subsequent revision. Although Freud himself was aware of the "two-way
nature of the seductiveness of the analytic situation" (Gabbard,
1996), recent papers tend to focus on the seduction theory rather
than seductions in the consulting room. They seem to refer either to
patients' relationships in their external world or to childhood
sexual abuse (Blass & Simon, 1994; Blum, 1996; Eissler, 1993; Garcia,
1987; Greenberg, 2001; Halberstadt-Freud, 1996; Laplanche, 1995,
1997; Tansey, 1994). However, in this chapter, I am writing about the
themes of seduction and betrayal (which seem to follow each other
just as night follows day) operating in the consulting room between
patient and analyst. To qualify this, I think betrayal is the inevitable
outcome of the experience of feeling seduced, although I would
acknowledge that betrayal can stand alone without a seduction
necessarily having taken place. Issues of revenge link with both
seduction and betrayal, as I try to illustrate with clinical material.
Both cases I shall discuss are men, but the issues I describe arise
equally with women patients.

It is important to be clear about the terms I am using here. "Seduction" is being used in its widest sense, according to the *Oxford English Dictionary*: seductive behaviour involves leading astray, tempting, enticing, alluring. In other words there may be erotic, sexual, or corruptive elements in a seductive encounter, but not necessarily so. However, I wish to stress that, in using the word "seduction", I am implying that some form of a "game" is being played out, either consciously or unconsciously. When seduction, in whatever way, is carried out by the analyst, then an enactment has taken place (Gerrard, 2007 and Chapter Seven). "Betrayal" implies something treacherous or disloyal. I would add to this the breaking of an expectation, hope, or implied promise. Again, here, this could include the sexual infidelity of the loved other, but I am using it in a wider context.

The ubiquitous nature of seduction and betrayal

As Freud observed, every child experiences seduction and betrayal in the natural course of development. As an example, I shall give a brief observation of a three-year-old girl, Sophie. On Saturday evenings, she loves to watch *Strictly Come Dancing* with her daddy, who has agreed to marry her when she is older. Father and daughter dress up and dance joyously together. This is fantasy, symbolic play, and as such can be totally delicious. Later, Sophie will be put to bed and accept that the rest of the evening belongs to her parents, although she may feel moments of betrayal, and quite possibly have a temper tantrum along the way. Here we have an instance of a wonderful mutual seduction—an Oedipal triumph for Sophie to relish.

These themes of seduction and betrayal feature in ancient and modern scenarios. In the Bible, for instance, we have the narratives of Adam and Eve, through to Samson and Delilah and then, in the New Testament, to Jesus and Judas. There is also a frequent focus in the plays of Shakespeare, in operatic works, and in art and literature generally, on issues of seduction and betrayal. By way of example, I will consider, briefly, the Puccini opera, *Madame Butterfly*.

A young, innocent girl, "Butterfly", is wooed by Pinkerton, an American naval officer visiting her town of Nagasaki. Prior to the wedding, he has confided in the American Consul that he hopes one day to have a "real" American wife. Thus, the audience is made aware early on in the opera of Pinkerton's intended betrayal. (However, there is an irony in that Butterfly herself has also been regarded by her family as the betrayer, because she renounced her religious faith, the faith of her forefathers, in order to embrace her husband's religion.) After marriage, they live together for a short while in what is assumed to be sexual bliss, before Pinkerton sets sail again for the USA. Following this, for the next three years, during which time their son is born, Butterfly sits waiting faithfully for his promised return. She alone, among all those around her, keeps faith and trust in her husband.

When she learns the truth in a heartbreaking scene where she sees that Pinkerton is now married to someone else and all that is left to her is to return to her previous life as a Geisha or to die, she relinquishes her son to Pinkerton and his wife and kills herself with her father's sword. We have seen that Pinkerton's ruthless sense of reality (intended seduction and betrayal) is in striking contrast to Butterfly's determined fantasy (unwittingly betrayed). In this case, the loss and disillusionment are so severe that they can only be tempered by death.

This opera, which rarely leaves a dry eye in the audience, is powerfully reflective of these universal themes of seduction and betrayal. I think that we are all deeply affected by the emotions aroused just because they are so primitive, emerging as they do out of early Oedipal constellations.

Theoretical and clinical aspects of seduction and betrayal

Caper (1998) comments on a Panel Discussion on "Seduction" held in Barcelona. He notes the different emphases that the papers placed on the origins of seduction. Some discussants focused on the inner void that leads to seducing or being available for seduction. Others stressed that the origin of seduction was in the experience of having been first seduced and then abandoned by the mother. My own view is that, in this case, seduction is fuelled by revenge. I do not think the experience of an inner void, which seduction tries to fill with momentary excitement, negates the revenge theory or vice versa. My sense is that, in all probability, both fuel the act of seduc-tion. I would stress, however, that, in my view, seduction has little to do with real desire. It is predominantly associated with control, conquest, revenge, and excitement, although, of course, it may have an important role in sexual fantasies.

Moving on to "betrayal", patients can feel betrayed by us when we are not attuned, misunderstand, or misrepresent them. Charles, in a paper entitled "Betrayal", has identified this as the analyst's unwillingness to engage in truth. She goes even further when she says, "We betray the patient to whom we cannot, out of intended kindness, acknowledge some weakness" (1997, p. 116). Charles refers to the real betrayal as being the denial of the patient's reality (akin to what we know of the mothers of hysterics), and this may arise from some sort of "blindness" on the part of the analyst. Some may consider that this could be carrying the notion of betrayal too far. However, in a chapter on seduction, Bollas (2000) writes of the deep harm that can be done during analysis when an analyst both fails to take up the sexual nature of a patient's material and fails to see clearly his/her own or the patient's seductiveness.

A paper by Josephs (2006) tackled the impulse to infidelity as a defence against the feelings of sexual betrayal by a partner, but, as he focused on the patient's external world, we are left not knowing whether seduction and betrayal were manifest in the consulting room between patient and analyst. This is the gap in much of the literature that I am addressing in this chapter, while acknowledg-ing the difficulty of such writing, which touches on enactments (Chapter Seven), erotic transferences and countertransferences (see also Chapters Four and Five), and even the possibility of boundary violations (Gabbard & Lester, 1995).

The difficulties in exploring these themes further within the analytic relationship is that, in certain cases, the analyst's empathy and understanding may be felt by the patient as a seduction (Bollas, 2000; Davies, 1998b). Another case scenario could be that the patient sees the analyst as someone who engenders trust so that the patient will let his/her guard down, but then is left vulnerable to a future betrayal (Josephs, 2001). In similar vein, Greenberg (2001) reminds us that Freud (1931b), in his paper on "Female sexu-ality", referred to the mother as the "seductress", and Greenberg suggests that in the analytic sphere, offering oneself as an object by providing satisfaction is a kind of seduction: "Every child is seduced into human relatedness itself" (2001, p. 424).

Oedipal and post-Oedipal dilemmas underpin these deep and difficult feelings that recur between patient and analyst. Davies (1994, 1998a,b, 2003) stresses the role of the parent "as a full participant in the erotic oedipal situation" (1994, p. 156) and explores fully in her papers the concept of post-Oedipal adult sexuality. She cites the differences between Oedipal and post-Oedipal. From the Oedipal sphere, she says, comes the

> passion and intensity born of an illusion of romantic perfection and deep, mutual idealization. But from the post-oedipal . . . comes the capacity to tolerate imperfections in our love objects, to experience disappointment with the death of desire, to apprehend that true intimacy requires mutual vulnerability and psychic interpenetration. [2003, p. 6]

This, says Davies, cannot happen without mutual recognition, reciprocal desire, and subsequent mourning by both analyst and patient.

I would stress here, and throughout this chapter, the central place that mourning has in working through. I am not suggesting that anything static or permanent takes place in a move from Oedipal to post-Oedipal, but I am adding to the notions of pre-Oedipal and Oedipal, that of the post-Oedipal—a more developed state of mind. Searles (1959a) also alluded to this post-Oedipal stage, suggesting that the end of the Oedipal romance is signalled by the child being able to recognize a "greater limiting reality" (p. 302).

Davies's thesis is that the Oedipus complex is not simply lost, but optimally both "won and lost" (Davies, 2003), as the child, who is the object of the parents' adoring love, experiences moments of Oedipal victory. I hope to show, through use of clinical material, that this transient victory is essential to the patient's sense of a lovable self.

In normal development, adolescents turn away from their parents towards other love relationships. Davies stresses that the danger in analysis can be that we are prone to interpret this turning away as "resistance", possibly not recognizing it for the developmental achievement that it may be: a move towards a post-Oedipal transference, involving the undoing of the adoring love affair and the mutual achievement of mourning (Davies, 2003). At the end of an analysis, the aim is for there to be a predominant state of "sexual aliveness and vitality" in the work, mourning what cannot be but maintaining hope for all that is possible (Davies, 1998a, p. 751).

There is the potential for issues of seduction and betrayal to arise and fester malignantly when these processes do not get worked through. Importantly, Davies (1998b) also distinguishes between "benign" and "malignant" seductiveness, the "malignant" being a disowning of desire on the part of the seducer, thus inducing a state of humiliation in the other. Seduction may encompass all types of desire, the negation of which can result in a malignant betrayal. The work of analysis is to tease out benign wishes and fantasies from those of a more disturbed or malignant nature. For example, a patient may experience his/her analyst as sexually alive and misinterpret this as seduction. I will illustrate this later, when I write of Sam.

Patients may try to seduce their analysts: it is their right to do so. As Betty Joseph said, "The patient has every right to try to seduce the analyst. The analyst has no right to allow himself to be seduced" (personal communication, 2001, cited in Gabbard, 2003, p. 257). Davies (1994) feels differently, in that she stresses the importance for the analyst of being able to participate symbolically, thus, at times, allowing the patient moments of Oedipal victory. Later, I shall illustrate this with clinical material about Alex, where, at times, I felt that I was the seductress. With both Sam and Alex, issues of seduction and betrayal pervaded the analytic encounter.

Laplanche (1997), who gives ". . . a kind of essential primacy to 'seduction'", says,

> It is the intervention enigmatically of the adult sexual unconscious into the perceptual realm of the infant that is the principal driving force of all scenes of seduction, and this is what renders the issue of seduction so fundamental. [quoted in Williams, 1998, p. 206]

Davies, who, as I said earlier, posits the parent as a "full participant in the erotic oedipal situation", albeit using different language, is, nevertheless, thinking in a similar way.

So, here we have a mix-up of a two-person relationship whose constituent factors are seduction and betrayal. For instance, Josephs (2001) writes of the fantasy experience of the infant who believes he has won an exclusive relationship with the desired parent, having defeated the rival, and then is shocked to discover the primal scene—his proof of betrayal. The excitement and power of Oedipal victory are subsequently dashed by reality, and herein lies the nub of psychological development. These themes are alive and operative in the following clinical material with Sam and Alex.

Clinical material

Sam

Sam (whom I have written about elsewhere (see Chapter Seven)) displayed a manifest eroticized transference from the beginning of a long treatment, most of which took place at five times weekly. Even in his first session on the couch, I was invited to engage in mutual oral sex with him. Much of his material, especially in the first few years, contained covert and overt invitations to his home, his bedroom, his bathroom, my bedroom, and many thoughts about how he could seduce me.

He alternated between assuming he was desirable and extreme self-deprecation—"who would want me?" In a session where he became aroused through his sexual talk and sexual fantasies, which also involved imagining me as a willing participant at a sex party ("a greedy girls' night"), he wondered if perhaps the attraction between us was not just one way. I realized that he confused my acceptance of him and his sexuality as my sexual desire for him. There was such a fine line in his mind between who was the seducer/seductress, and which of us, in the event of our not getting it together sexually, would be the betrayer or betrayed.

Sam was the only child of a drunken, violent father and a depressed and emotionally absent mother and his early experiences resulted in his borderline functioning. He was much more comfortable with his murderous rage and hatred than with relationships of a loving nature, although he had developed a loving relationship with a young nephew. His "love" for, or attachment to, me was expressed in his efforts to seduce me and possess me, thus winning an Oedipal victory over my husband.

I shall illustrate this with an explicit fantasy of Sam's just prior to a holiday break, and then examine the roots of this fantasy. He would lie naked and erect on the couch. I would find him irresistible and would "sit" on him and we would gaze into each other's eyes, full of passion and excitement. After forty-five minutes we would have an ecstatic mutual orgasm and then he would get dressed and leave. This, he said, we could repeat at every session.

Besides sexualizing the relationship he was about to lose because of the forthcoming break, and burying his murderous hatred in perverse thoughts, he was also expressing his craving for the adoring gaze of the absent mother. My hypothesis with Sam—born out of reconstruction and memory—was that he had never been the adored, idealized object of his mother's Oedipal interest and love (Kohut's "gleam in his mother's eye" (1966, p. 252). As Davies (2003) confirms:

> The failure to relinquish and mourn is predicated on an earlier frustration of the developmental need to be adored and, to possess, to exist, for one perfect moment in time, in full possession of and awareness of the parent's idealized romantic interest; and to dwell there long enough and fully enough to contemplate having had enough and moving beyond it. [p. 13]

I believe that Sam captured this wish within this explicit sexual fantasy.

As his analysis progressed, Sam had to face the failure of his frequent attempts to seduce me. He seemed to lose interest in what was on offer and began to talk of money worries, of having had enough of analysis, and wanting to end. Our termination was gradual, over a period of two years, as there were certainly many issues to deal with, including his rarely owned attachment to me. However, I realized in hindsight that Sam probably did not achieve what he needed during his analysis with me. Perhaps he experienced an analyst who was not seducible enough, for he did not arouse the erotic countertransference feelings that would be the equivalent of the mother's adoring gaze. I was not "seduced" when perhaps I needed to have been. If this had been experienced by me, not necessarily interpreted in any way, but recognized consciously in the countertransference, the patient might have felt more positive about his capacity to charm and seduce. Instead, there were hopeless, empty attempts to entice me. In Chapter Four, I have written about patients needing to find their analysts' loving feelings at some point during their analysis. Now I am coming to the realization that perhaps also each patient has to find that there are moments when his analyst has felt seduced by his charms and found him desirable. This accords with Mann's (1999) concept of a good enough erotic transference and countertransference, and underlines Davies's proposition that the Oedipal victory is both "won and lost". Of course, if some form of seduction is experienced, then betrayal inevitably follows, but I believe that much of the work with patients, especially those who eroticize their relationship with their analyst and sexualize their hatred, is to work through these themes time and again.

The final ending with Sam was very painful, albeit I only learned just how painful after we had parted. He got up from the couch and moved towards me to give me a hug. I resisted this by putting what I felt to be a restraining hand on his shoulder and suggesting that we shake hands. His move towards me came as a surprise, although, having been aware of problematic endings with other therapists, it should not have done so. I subsequently received a letter with his final cheque, letting me know that he was still recovering from the "injury" to his shoulder and that I may be hearing from his solicitors. I responded to this letter acknowledging how painfully rejected he had felt but also reminding him of the valuing comments he had made to me prior to the ending. I did not hear from him further.

I think Sam had been left feeling utterly betrayed, and not solely because of the unconsummated hug. Although I could not put right what had felt wrong, I did come to realize that my "rejecting" reaction represented an understandable countertransference response. Davies (2003) writes of the analyst who may be terrified by the patient's demands and, thus, unconsciously perhaps, moves "away from the patient's wished-for response and inexorably closer to what looks like the original parental deadness or narcissistic preoccupation" (p. 14). This captures my experience of being with Sam in the last few months of our work together.

Alex

Seduction and betrayal took a somewhat different form with Alex, a patient who had been in five times-weekly analysis for some years. A significant element in his infantile history was that he was the second son born to a mother who desperately wanted a daughter (for complex reasons that I cannot cite here). She exemplified the rather typical mother of a hysteric, as described by Bollas (2000): one who cannot celebrate her infant's body. She may compensate for not being available as a mentalizing object by offering herself as a sensual object, making believe that there are no problems and everything is fine. Brenman (1985b) has suggested that the mother of a male hysteric unconsciously conveys to her son a sense of impending catastrophe. To counteract these feelings, she may well be over-protective and over-attentive. Alex's father was described as a somewhat ineffectual, rather weak man. These factors seem to have set the scene for seduction and betrayal. My experience of Alex in the consulting room has accorded with the features that lead to a diagnosis of hysterical personality disorder. There are many papers on hysterical personality disorder (Bell, 1992; Bollas, 2000; Brenman, 1985b; Britton, 1999; Chodoff, 1978; Easser & Lesser, 1965; Lionells, 1986—to name but a few). Areas of agreement on the defining characteristics of these patients include: being troubled by the body's sexual demands; a self-image of inauthenticity; a high degree of overt emotionality and theatricality; chronic dissatisfaction and a sense of incompleteness, leading to a search to be loved and desired; apparent seductiveness. Most writers would agree with Brenman (1985b) that the hysteric's wish is to be "the falsely adored object of love and to triumph over so-called loving objects who are then despised and annihilated" (p. 424).

Brenman (1985b) emphasizes the "persuasive propaganda" in hysteria to prove that a certain condition is true. He stresses the negation of psychic reality, illustrating this with the "Don Juan syndrome":

> Freud (1893–95) considered that in hysteria there is a stalemate tug-of-war between sexuality and repression. The Don Juan manages to achieve a pseudosexuality at the service of his narcissistic conquest. He uses external objects to persuade them of his supremacy and lives through his imagined picture of himself inside his objects. [p. 423]

As illustrated below, Alex exhibited many of these hysterical characteristics, including the Don Juan tendency.

Alex (whom I have also written about previously (Gerrard, 2004, and Chapter Seven)) quickly demonstrated a yearning relationship towards me, was consumed by desires for me and the sessions, yet, at the same time, tortured himself with the idea that I would find him despicable. In the sessions he was very vocal—bellows of rage and agonized screams reflected his anger, desire, and frustration as well as somatic symptoms of headache and gutache. There were moments, too, when Alex's expression of feelings of hurt, humiliation, and/or rage created a sexually charged atmosphere. I needed to consider my own experiences of sexual arousal in relation to both Alex's eroticization of his primitive needs (i.e., as in the case of many hysterics, the wish for maternal care that has become sexualized) and my sadistic triumph in response to my patient's masochism (Field, 1989). In the context of seduction and betrayal, I came to understand this as something to do with experiencing moments of having been "seduced" by Alex. At these moments, my body, like his, spoke and responded to his need to be desired. Communications from Alex regarding his "certainty" that I did not want him triggered in me a desire to reassure (see also Chapter Seven). Sometimes, then, I experienced my patient as the seducer, but, at other times, I found myself in this role. For instance, once he said during an evening session that, when he saw the lights on in my home, he knew I wanted to be with my family and not with him. I responded that the light in this room was on for him. Afterwards I felt that my statement had been seductive, but it had a transformative effect on Alex's affect for a while. He ceased to be quite so histrionic, became more realistic about my acceptance of him as one of my patients, towards whom I could maintain an interest, respect, and an "overall positive countertransference" (Britton, 2003). Perhaps the "light", not just in the house, but also in his analyst, shown through my care and acceptance of him, was indeed a reality.

I wondered, however, to what extent I had been unconsciously trying to deflect the hatred of me that lay behind his mask of self-hatred, and that my patient may have experienced my comment as a seductive enactment. This was confirmed some weeks later when Alex let me know that he had felt rather betrayed by my response.

He said my comment had "checkmated" him. It appeared that he felt I had headed off his rage, so that for the time being he had nowhere to go with what was felt to be my reassuring seductiveness.

This sequence of seduction followed by betrayal is, to my mind, inevitably right at the core of the working through that needs to happen within the pre-Oedipal and Oedipal transference. Seductive interventions by the analyst constitute some form of "enactment". Indeed, in Chapter Seven, on "Enactments", I suggest that many hysterical patients induce rescue fantasies in the analyst and, thus, her interventions with these patients may become seductive. She may tend to rescue both herself and her patients from their rage and sadism. However, when patients experience seduction by their analyst and subsequently feel a sense of betrayal, what is likely to follow is a wish for revenge. This quote from Steiner is as relevant here as it was in Chapter Three:

> The sense of wrong experienced is made more painful if it follows a period of seduction by the primary object, who may have colluded in fostering the belief that oedipal intimacy is desired by the mother as well as the child. The result is that when this fantasy collapses the child feels that a promise has been broken, so that he is not only wronged but betrayed. It is often at this point that the demand for justice turns to the thirst for vengeance. [1996, p. 435]

I am positing in this chapter that, for many patients, moments of experience of Oedipal triumph in having seduced their analyst are vital. However, since these moments are transitory, disappointment, frustration, betrayal, and revenge can subsequently emerge and, one hopes, be more fully understood.

Lionells (1986) spells out the themes that emerge in working with the inner world of the hysteric: (1) his chronic need and desire; (2) a recognition that what he seeks from his object is love, affection, and approval; (3) his object is enticed, controlled, or manipulated into fulfilling his needs. I found these themes constantly operating in my work with Alex. While seduction and betrayal issues are ubiquitous and arise frequently in reworking Oedipal issues, they are more particularly core issues to the whole personality and mode of functioning in the hysteric.

At one point, some years into our work, I identified to Alex what I named as his "Don Juan" tendencies (Brenman, 1985b; Lubbe, 2003). I had been aware of this mode of functioning for some time based on his description of various relationships in his external world—in particular, his dealings with women. Although, in the transference, I was meant to be both admiring and jealous, we had reached a stage where I felt that, with a growing sense of external reality and a more real self, he could deal with the challenge of taking this on board. Earlier on, he was too narcissistically fragile to have done so. His immediate response to my Don Juan interpretation was of fury with me, denying his cruelty or wish for revenge on women. Over time, and with much hard work in sessions, he accepted and understood that there was another "him" who sought revenge on his mother by "loving and leaving" women. Although he had to deal with the other's sense of betrayal as he "backed off", I think that Alex, too, felt betrayed. Seducing, achieving his goal of being passionately loved and desired, and then finding a temporary sense of triumph was followed by feelings of betrayal, because the expected promise of a love so engulfing that it could resolve the internal empty state did not materialize.

Revenge is expressed *in* the seduction and then arises *as a consequence of* the betrayal. When Alex felt that he was not the centre of my life, he could sometimes become vengeful and attacking. One such time was when he thought he spotted my husband in the front garden carrying a grandchild. What followed was a diatribe about the apocalyptic state of the world and everything being so futile and hopeless with our planet. This material, carefully unpicked, revealed his vengeful attack on my grandchildren and the analysis, which was felt to be useless, particularly as this had occurred just prior to a summer break. During breaks, when he could feel totally abandoned, Alex was more likely to become involved in relationships with women so that he could re-establish himself as the object of desire.

There was a very deep feeling that, if he was not my only special one, then he was nobody and we all may as well be dead. The Don Juan tendencies served to stave off the knowledge of reality and ordinariness, as well as providing a way of revenging himself against mother/women who seduce and betray. Alex had adopted the role of seducer to endeavour to get supremacy and control of his objects. Sometimes, his Don Juan role was employed to combat Oedipal rivalry with my husband; at others, to become in fantasy the child/grandchild who is held adoringly in the arms of a parent/grandparent/analyst. Thus, Alex veered between his pre-Oedipal and Oedipal needs and desires.

There were times when I became "seduced" into Alex's way of seeing things (Brenman's (1985b) "persuasive propaganda"). For example, for a while, when he talked about being "kicked out" at the end of sessions, I went along with this notion, interpreting the pain of being sent away, not being in control, and somehow understanding that this "kicking out" was an expression of my lack of love for him. After some further thinking, I was able to distance myself from this notion and came back to my reality: I did not "kick him out", but our session came to an end. This allowed me to disentangle myself from the role of heartless persecutor, and Alex from the role of victim. Exclusion is the common factor in Alex's struggles, which takes us straight back to the primal scene and Britton's understanding of the hysteric who "gets in on the act" (1999). The following passage describes Alex's difficulties in this realm very well: "in hysteria the insistence is on possessing exclusively the analyst's love, leading to a transference 'illusion' that ignores the importance of any other reality than love and annihilates the analyst's erotic bonds with anyone else" (Britton, 1999, p. 11).

Lionells (1986) spells out the task of treatment: the need to recognize the processes of attachment and detachment which can slowly be replaced by more genuine relating, and the aim that "rage gives way to genuine anger, whining demandingness to clear assertion, clinging dependency to mutuality, and finally, manipulative need may be replaced by the capacity to love" (p. 12). These aims were gradually met in the work with Alex, which I would like to illustrate with a vignette from his analysis.

He paid me a somewhat reduced fee because of his circumstances and the frequency of sessions. I then discovered that he had spent a considerable amount of money on some luxury items. I felt that I had been seduced into a lower fee, and the "entitled" patient came to mind (see Chapter Three). As tactfully as I could, I tried to tackle this anomaly with him. He endeavoured at a surface level to take this on board but, unconsciously, he felt utterly betrayed and abused by me, as if I had called him a liar and a cheat. For a while, psychosomatic symptoms took the place of a capacity to vent his rage.

Then, following a dream where, manifestly, difficult issues arose with a female employer, Alex got closely in touch with his rage with me. He suddenly bellowed, "It's none of your goddamn business what I spend my money on. If you want to put up your fees, then you should do so and I will find a way to pay them." I rejoiced in this response to me, which contained genuine anger, clear assertion, mutuality, and the capacity to love. Because of the authenticity and spontaneity of his response, my reaction to my patient was a very loving one; once Alex had expressed himself so cleanly and clearly, he felt a more genuine love towards me as well (Chapter Four). Following on from this, issues of his false self and capacity for real expression of feelings were addressed, so that gradually it became possible for Alex to abandon some of his more entrenched hysterical defence mechanisms.

Conclusion

As I have demonstrated, both in the work with my patients and in the observation of Sophie, I believe that moments of seduction and Oedipal victory are essential to our post-Oedipal psychic well-being. While the vignette about Sophie is wholly joyous, it is important to stress the absolute necessity that disillusionment must follow the wonderful illusion of Oedipal triumph. Father and daughter have jointly created a fantasy that has later to be dispelled.

The reality for patients is that, while they may indulge in rare moments of feeling seductive and special, they have to face that their analyst does not belong to them, has her own life and love objects, raises her fees, and terminates the sessions on time. This reality may well result in a sense of betrayal and a wish for revenge. Indeed, in the early stages of analyses, how could it not do so? Patients will inevitably find these Oedipal issues reactivated in the course of their analysis (Rusbridger, 2004) and the wish for revenge is the natural outcome of seduction and betrayal. As Steiner says, Oedipal issues trigger "a deep sense of injustice and violation that fuels the wish for revenge" (1996, p. 435). In the cases I have described, the repetitive erotic yearnings for what cannot be were expressed by seductive behaviour leading to the all too familiar sense of betrayal.

Analysis needs to offer opportunities for "Oedipal injustice", revenge, and mourning to be experienced, so that resentment can be replaced with forgiveness (Steiner, 1996).

In the case of Sam, this mourning stage could not be achieved, in part because his Oedipal trauma was re-enacted between us in a way that could not be worked through. Some of my learning from that case enabled me to contain Alex's Oedipal re-enactments in such a way that we could experience them together and then mourn their passing. While seduction and betrayal are features likely to arise in all analyses, I have suggested that in patients with hysterical personalities, such as Alex, these issues are intensified between patient and analyst.

Tansey (1994) has suggested that, ever since Breuer's ill-advised treatment of Anna O and Jung's sexual entanglement with Sabina Spielrein, issues of erotic transferences and seduction have pro-duced a "phobic dread" in many psychoanalysts. This is reflected, as I have discovered, by the relative paucity of literature on the subject. Based on my own experience, I would advocate a sharper awareness of seduction and betrayal issues in the consulting room than I believe has been the case generally. I hope I have conveyed the importance of being keenly attuned to the seductive inter-changes, which in some cases are just nuances, and in others are full-blown declarations of sexual desire or love.

I have also suggested that towards the end of an analysis, at times, post-Oedipal states of mind may be achieved where patient and analyst have mourned what cannot be but still carry hope for what is possible (Davies, 1998a). These more mature states of mind herald a time where the psychic "games" of seduction and betrayal, followed by revenge, are behaviours of the past. When the distinc-tion between fantasy and reality is generally well established, patients may safely bask in the knowledge that, very occasionally during their analyses, they have truly captivated their analyst in moments such as Sophie experienced with her daddy on Saturday nights.

PART III

CHALLENGES TO THE PSYCHOTHERAPEUTIC FRAME

Enactments in the countertransference (with special reference to rescue fantasies with hysterical patients)

I n this chapter, I describe enactments in the countertransference, spanning fantasies, actions, words, and sexual responses to patients. The origins and reverberations of the analyst's enactments are explored in an effort to understand whether they have obstructed progress or created special moments in the therapy where shifts in the patients' inner world, or further understanding on the part of the analyst, could occur.

I illustrate my themes with clinical vignettes from work with several patients, although I will focus mainly on work with patients who present with hysterical personality. The chapter is an endeavour to tease out what, if any, differences there may be in working with hysterical patients, as opposed to patients with other personality types, in the nature of countertransference enactments. I shall examine the role of rescue fantasies in the creation of an enactment.

According to Renik, "there aren't enactments (plural); there is only enactment (singular), a constant, unavoidable aspect of everything patient and analyst do in analysis" (1997, p. 281). Jacobs, likewise, writing about "subtle, often scarcely visible countertransference reactions" (1986, p. 289) says, "aspects of the very interpretive process itself may imperceptibly have become an enactment"

(1986, p. 306). Steiner (2006), writing twenty years later, also agrees that interpretations themselves can represent an enactment and stresses the importance of self-observation. Gabbard concurs, stating, "countertransference enactments are ubiquitous, probably unavoidable, and potentially useful" (1994, p. 1083). This seems to be the prevailing consensus from both classical and relational psychoanalysts, at least since Sandler's now seminal 1976 paper, "Countertransference and role-responsiveness". See also Chused (1991); Davies (1994); Field (1989); Frayn (1993); Hoffman (1983); Jacobs (1986); Levenson (2006); McLaughlin (1991); Renik (1997); Schwaber (1992); Tuckett (1997).

I find my reading and research here helpful. As long as I can free myself from the punitive superego that says "you shouldn't have done/said that", then I can find the curiosity and wish to understand so that I can ask myself the question "I wonder why you did/said that?"

In order to be clear about the nature of countertransference enactment, I will state briefly what has probably been stated many times before: an enactment is jointly created by the unconscious of patient and analyst. It is distinguished from *projective identification* in that the analyst's own transferences are activated in enactment (McLaughlin, 1991) and from ordinary *countertransference* in that during an enactment the analyst's capacity for observation is clouded. Chused (1991), Steiner (2006), and Gabbard and Lester (1995) distinguish enactments from *violations*, whereby violations are not subject to analytic scrutiny by the analyst in which any possible harm to the patient could be understood psychoanalytically.

Enactment through fantasy

In an earlier paper (1990) I wrote of a countertransference enactment with a female patient, who had been sexually abused. I called her "A", although in this chapter I shall call her Mary. (I would now describe this patient as one with a predominantly hysterical personality.) I found myself in the grip of a recurring fantasy. I became transfixed by my wish to see my patient's genitalia. That was my principal wish—not to touch, just to look. I began to work hard on myself. Was this an, as yet, undiscovered homosexual part of me, or an aspect of my patient, or was it something else altogether? I quote from the paper:

> I thought that if this fantasy were carried through, A (Mary) would be humiliated by me, she would lose her (very fragile) trust in me, I would have abandoned her as a therapist—she would be altogether abused. But for moments in her therapy I was only able to see her as a sexual object to be used—no abused—for my own pleasure. I was stuck at Winnicott's third stage in the process of The Use of an Object . . .—i.e. in danger of destroying her as an analytic object/patient of mine and it was necessary to do some hard work in my mind so that we could proceed to where she as object survives my destructive counter-transference fantasies, and I can re-use her as a patient. [Gerrard, 1990, p. 123]

Later on in the therapy, she increased the number of weekly sessions, and I began to understand how this sexualized wish of mine to "see" was symbolic of the need to see into her, see beyond the "outer clothing", and understand more fully this (hysterical) patient's way of sexualizing her infantile needs. Another way of understanding this, and perhaps more relevant to this paper, would be using Sandler's theory of role-responsiveness (1976). Mary's mother may well have been repelled by her genitals, as evidenced in theories of mothers of female hysterics (Bollas, 2000, and Chapter Six). Certainly she had reported that her mother seemed to find anything of a sexual nature quite disgusting. I think that perhaps in our dyad, unconsciously, Mary needed a therapist who could love and admire her genitalia and that I was nudged into the role. I may also have represented for Mary an aspect of herself in relation to her mother—a curious child in the presence of a "covered up" mother.

This was an early, very powerful and persistent countertransference enactment which, albeit difficult to allow and process in myself at the time, offered me a profound respect for such experiences and the value they offer to the analyst who can resist "acting" and wait for understanding to emerge.

Later still, in the therapy I found myself in another "enactment", in that I responded too promptly to her sense of isolation between Wednesdays and Fridays and offered a Thursday session. Subsequently, Mary was moved to tears, feeling that she had been "picked up and carried" as opposed to mother's way of soothing, which she pictured as "jiggling the pram with her hip". However, quite understandably, this enactment did not assuage deep feelings of loneliness and mistrust that I would still drop her, find her too much or too heavy to hold (Gerrard, 2000).

This is an example of what I want to propose in this Chapter. Patients with hysterical type personality seem to elicit a particular kind of "rescuing fantasy and subsequent enactment" in the analyst.

I shall demonstrate this in later clinical examples, and endeavour to show that this type of enactment does not seem to occur with patients of other personality types, such as narcissistic or borderline.

Enactment through action

I would like to cite here two vignettes showing how enactments on my part involved actual physical movements during sessions. The first, described in Chapter Two, "Spaces in between", concerned my patient, Jean. I wrote in detail of my physical movements in the session, leaving my chair to change the page on the calendar and then again to put on the electric heater. In hindsight, it seems to me quite an extreme countertransference enactment on my part. I must have been trying hard to show Jean that I was human during a time when it was very difficult to establish a meaningful connection. At the time, my understanding was about my physical movement triggering her psychic movement. Her image of me changed, and with it her resistance toward me lessened, so that she looked across the room at me and said, "Hello, Jackie Gerrard." The full vignette is described in Chapter Two, and it seemed to be a pivotal moment in our relationship.

The second vignette is taken from an earlier paper, "Ocnophilia and the interpretation of transference" (2000), and is about a patient whom I called Susan. Her history involved a prolonged separation from her mother when she was barely two years old. Mother had given birth to a new sibling and left the country for a while, taking the new baby with her. During the early years of therapy, Susan, naturally experienced intense feelings over separation.

In the session following one where I had given her the dates of a forthcoming break, she was feeling very young, vulnerable and tearful. She spoke of the fact that two weeks felt like six months but was, at the same time, able to verbalize what she wanted to say "take me with you". Her feelings were of intense pain and anger and produced thoughts (for her) such as: I could not really care, she obviously was not important to me, did I understand how much she needed me? Suddenly I recalled that I had put something on to cook in the kitchen and had forgotten to switch off the hob. I was taken over with thoughts and images of my house burning down, of destruction of my home and consulting room—to the extent that I could no longer focus on my patient. It is exceptionally rare that I would leave a session, but at that moment I felt I had to do so. I told my patient that I recognized this was a very painful time for her, especially as we were so involved with the difficulties for her of being left, but I thought I had omitted to attend to something in the kitchen which necessitated my leaving the room. I would only be a few moments. Imagine my horror when I found that I had, after all, switched off the hotplate. I returned seconds later to a patient who said that she would rather the house had burned down, that she had wanted the clock to stop. I came to understand this as a feeling that she could not go on living without me at that moment, and if necessary we should be destroyed together. I had to do some hard work on myself and my countertransference feelings and acting out (enactment). The message I had received was certainly along the lines that I could not bear the intensive needs, wishes and clinging responses of my patient to my break. I was allowed to know in a very deep way about the extent of Susan's ocnophilic wishes through this most unusual occurrence. Following on from this, I had to find a way to interpret to her the depth of these within our relationship as she became more ready to hear them for herself. . . . My holiday break and my subsequent leaving her alone in the consulting room were temporarily felt to be traumatic experiences for Susan but, fortunately in time, the understanding of these events, together with her, and in myself, re-established the frame and took Susan forward in her therapy. She commented subsequently that she had felt that particular session to be very important indeed despite the acute pain it produced. [Gerrard, 2000, p. 408]

I have quoted from this last vignette at length, as I feel this is a good example of the nature of countertransference enactment that took the form of physical movement. There followed from this a great deal of progress in understanding for both of us of the early unbearable and almost wordless trauma. I understood the pressure in me to leave the room at that time, with the accompanying images of fire and destruction, as a countertransference expression of the intense fear of a catastrophe. Maybe, although we had addressed Susan's fearful and clinging behaviour many times before, it was only when I, too, became swamped with terrors of catastrophe (which I had perhaps resisted until then) that I could know the full extent of these in my patient.

In terms of the rescue fantasy that I mentioned earlier, neither Jean nor Susan was of a hysterical personality type. I realize that my movements with Jean could be seen to be a kind of rescuing, and yet, I think it was more about my own need to prove my "ordinary humanity" to my patient.

A third vignette, illustrating "action", albeit with less emphasis on actual physical movement, concerns a patient, Lisa, who was in intensive therapy with me. I have come to understand her as being of a hysterical personality type. During a session when she had come into the consulting room while the weather was dry, a torrential thunderstorm developed. It was bucketing with rain as the session ended and she was wearing a thin dress. I found myself thinking quickly. I recalled Nina Coltart writing once about a case where an analyst saw his/her patient who arrived dripping wet. I think Dr Coltart was discussing "manners"—an important topic of hers. She wrote, almost sarcastically, about the analyst, wondering why he/she did not give the patient a towel. This was at the forefront of my mind as my patient got up from the couch. Also, I knew my umbrella was in the car, not in the house. I suggested to her if she would like to wait a moment, I would give her a towel to protect her while she got to her car, and she could return it to me the next session. I did so.

I subsequently gave myself a hard time, with the familiar "you shouldn't have done that", even imagining myself being found out and struck off! I knew that it was not disastrous to send my patient out without the towel and yet the "rescue fantasy" took hold. She would experience me as particularly thoughtful, humane, and kind.

The repercussions of the enactment here were that Lisa brought my towel back (she did not report me to the Ethics Committee) and said she had felt warmly mothered and cared for. As she often clung to a belief that I could not stand her, this could be viewed as a corrective experience. However, a fuller understanding would surely encompass my wish to have a grateful patient, rather than an unhappy and often raging and destructive one. An alternative scenario, of course, was that I could have done nothing (although possibly this would also have been an enactment) and let her return to the next session either furious, or resigned to the fact that, as she knew already, she could not expect anything more in the form of help, caring, or warmth from her primary object. I feel this is an example of an enactment that, of itself, did not prove to be of particular use in furthering the analysis of my patient, except that it did serve to increase my awareness of my *rescuing* impulses towards her.

Further discussion regarding the analyst's rescue fantasies

Hysterical patients, I believe, often had self-preoccupied and disinterested mothers, whom they did not feel held them in mind/internalized them: thus, they need to become what Bollas called "an event" (Bollas, 1987b).

Bollas (1987b) says,

> when the hysteric represents her state of mind through a dramatic use of self (first a sympathetic figure, then an anguished person, finally an enraged presence) she conveys to the analyst a particular impression: that of a *wretched* self. [p. 199]

Herein, I believe, is the source of the rescue fantasy that the analyst can entertain, and, indeed, as I did with Lisa, act upon. I have found very little reference in the literature to rescue fantasies, but Benjamin refers to these in different terms.

> It is noteworthy that Freud, in referring to what we now think of as the classical rules, does not distinguish between the analyst's countertransference fantasy of being a redeemer and the patient's fantasy of him as the savior in the transference. The countertransference fantasy reflects the analyst's disowned desire to be saved, which is projected onto the vulnerable, needy patient. It is this unconscious identification with the wish to be saved that stimulates

and colludes with the idealization, sometimes leading to enactment of the erotic transference in a dynamic very like that between Breuer and Anna. [Benjamin, 2001, p. 51]

She continues to spell out the dilemma for the analyst: if he sticks to the rule of "abstinence", is he any less the "redeemer"? The conflict can lead to an impasse. If we allow our personality to be available to our patients, does that tempt us to become redeemers? If we deny this and fall back on the rules, we may lose the opportunity that analysis affords us, even if enactments become the currency, to understand more fully the redeemer role that certain patients bestow on us. (My contention is that this is particularly so in the case of hysterics.) I think Benjamin's point regarding the wish to be saved as a disowned desire of the analyst is an important feature of countertransference enactments, emerging as they do from the analyst's unconscious.

Britton (2003) refers to Freud's 1910 paper, "A special type of choice of object made by men", defining "rescue phantasies". The subject is in identification with a parent (a woman is the mother rescuing her child, while a man is rescuing his mother), as Freud says, "the rescuer, in phantasy, becomes his or her own parent" (Freud, 1910h, quoted by Britton 2003, p. 53). Britton concludes "what is on offer to the analyst from the patient's erotic transference is the opportunity to see himself through her eyes, as a hero" (Britton, 2003, p. 54). Finally, Britton offers us another factor behind the need to rescue, which needs careful monitoring as it could also lead from a wish to an enactment, "the analyst's countertransference contains a feeling of obligation that is complementary to the patient's transference sense of entitlement" (*ibid.*, p. 56). Of course, obligation (coloured by guilt) may be very different to a more grandiose fantasy of being redeemer/rescuer/saviour, but this notion also reflects the complementary nature of the mutual participation that results in countertransference enactments.

Gabbard and Lester, in writing of both sexual and non-sexual boundary violations, are also stressing complementarity when they identify a common factor in a violation as the analyst's perception of a deficit in the patient. This, then, may provoke the analyst to assume the role of the idealized rescuer and "fill the void left by the patient's parenting experience" (1995, p. 120)

Enactment through use of words

I wish to illustrate here how I found myself using what some may feel is seductive language with a male patient whom I would classify as a hysteric. Two separate occasions come especially to mind. The first was earlier in the treatment of Alex, who was in five times-weekly analysis. (see Chapter Six). There was the time, described in the vignette in Chapter Six, when I said that the light in this room was on for him. This statement was, at the time, transformational, and he began to acknowledge something more realistic, much less histrionic, that the light, not perhaps just in the house, but in me through my care and acceptance of him, was indeed a reality. In encountering this hatred, turned on himself, I was reminded of Freud's paper "Mourning and melancholia" (1917e), and of the notion of the hysteric who hates his object but attacks himself instead. Were my words, I have often wondered, an effort to deflect the hatred of me that I felt was behind the mask of his self-hatred? Were they an important piece of reality to counteract my patient's unreal convictions? Either or both may be true. In any case, I think they were probably experienced by my patient as a seductive enactment, although they created some change and growth over time. Alex almost told me as much many months later, when he referred back to that session and said he felt I had "checkmated" him.

Time and again, the unconscious communication set up between my patient and myself is something like:

Alex: You don't love me.
Analyst: Of course I do.
Alex: Prove it then.
Analyst: All right, I will say something especially loving to you.

The second occurrence of this type of enactment occurred just before a break. Alex's self-esteem was by now much greater, with a considerable reduction of his grandiosity, and he had a firmer grip on reality. Nevertheless, he found himself feeling angry, hateful, and pining for something more from me at that particular time, just prior to a separation. He said very angrily that he did not just crave a hug; he could give really good hugs, too. I said rather quietly, "Yes, I know." This stopped Alex in his tracks, and he asked incredulously how I knew. He is a patient who had a good grasp of working within the symbolic arena, and I said that it was my experience that he had often given me a warm and appreciative hug through his responses. He began to cry and was much moved. Indeed, so was I, and again it was a rather transformational moment, yet I knew it also to be seductive and to have had the effect of stemming his rage. Had I "checkmated" him again, I wondered? Were we just back in a "you don't love me"; "yes I do" type of communication? I could certainly have spoken to him, as I had frequently, about the disappointing relationship he has with me whereby he finds himself short-changed, in the way he did repeatedly with both his parents. This had, at times, and could possibly on this occasion, have been productive. However, had I done so, would that have been another type of enactment—for instance, a "retreat" from the implications of the physical and sexual relationship (Schwaber, 1992)? Here we have the conflict referred to earlier quoted by Benjamin (2001), that of strict analytic technique *vs.* the analyst using something of herself. Both in their own way may constitute different types of enactments (McLaughlin, 1991). It is important to note here that my words to Alex would appear to be words that *rescue* him from the quagmire that is filled with his rage and desire.

Enactment through sexual response

Here, I want to illustrate from sexual material that arose in the therapy of two male patients, the first more borderline in his functioning and the other with a hysterical personality organization. The analyst's responses are very different in each case.

Sam (described in Chapter Six) displayed an eroticized transference from the beginning. In his first session on the couch, he reported that he was having an exciting fantasy of oral sex with me, where we were each stimulating the other. He veered between stated sexual desire and overtly sexually explicit language on the one hand, and infantile erotic need on the other. He found it hard to distinguish between his infantile and adult needs and desires as everything was sexualized.

In a session in the second year of analysis (fairly soon after he had realized my husband was now working from home, signified by another car in the driveway) he immediately commented that he liked my white blouse very much—in fact, he said, it really turned him on. It revealed my armpits, and he particularly liked women's armpits—he wanted to lick them. Then he said he felt like a teenager, but the feelings were not unpleasant. I felt sure he had an erection. He talked a good deal about sexual threesomes, sex parties, how he bottled out at the last minute of the "greedy girls night"—a sex party in my area, apparently, some years ago. He thought therapists who can talk so easily about sex are not necessarily disapproving of all that. I interpreted his excited wish to triumph over any man there may be in my life. I suggested that he was experiencing the difficulty in both wanting to be admired by his father but, at the same time, to triumph over him (based on much work we had done in this area). I also commented that perhaps he thought of me as the "greedy girl" wanting two men at the same time. I said that I thought he had become quite excited here today with me. He acknowledged that he was sexually aroused. He wondered, however, if the attraction here was not just one way. I said that I thought it was easy to confuse being accepted and appreciated with being sexually desired. I wondered if perhaps it stemmed from his not knowing if he wanted his mother's breasts and armpits as her child, or her vagina, as her lover (also based on previous work and my knowledge of the patient). Sam ended saying it had been a good session—he thought he would join a Keep Fit Club.

I have given this very sexually explicit vignette in order to demonstrate that sexual material of itself does not necessarily lead to sexual arousal in the analyst. Indeed my countertransference feelings were quite protective, of both Sam and myself, and I endeavoured to do just that. My principal wish was to offer containment in a set-up where I felt Sam could feel very uncontained.

Where some type of enactment may have taken place was in my *lack* of sexual desire. I was meant to be aroused, as he was, or, as Tuckett (1997) would have suggested, press-ganged into Sam's closed system. Was there perhaps on my part a resistance, a retreat to the "rules" as enactment? Or perhaps my "role-responsiveness" meant that I became the depressed and uninvolved mother Sam could not light up? In Sam's continual attempts to involve me, there are frequent incidents of acting out/in (Boesky, 1982). Acting out (or in) leaves the analyst as an observer of the experience, as opposed to a participant in it (Chused, 1991, Gabbard 1994), and this is mostly how it was with Sam.

Ogden (1996) illustrates how the perverse patient seeks to create excitement to counteract the inner experience of "dead parental intercourse" and, thereby, a lack of originality and spontaneity in the analysis. I found that, largely, my emotional participation came into play when my patient could identify with his infantile desires and then he evoked in me a warm, maternally erotic countertransference (Welles & Wrye, 1991).

Alex, whom I mentioned earlier (and also in Chapter Six), and who inhabits the psychic world of a male hysteric, demonstrated a yearning relationship towards me and was consumed with desire for me and the sessions. Over time, it became clearer that his core wish was to be the object of my desire. He tended to somatize his feelings, and he often reported backache, headaches, and gut-ache, which could appear and disappear with equal speed. He was also able to shout and scream and make his presence very much an "event" (Bollas, 1987b).

There were many moments when Alex expressed feelings of hurt, humiliation, and/or rage, during which there was an atmosphere of things being sexually charged in the room. Something sado-masochistic was operating, and the work was to try to understand these sexualized moments in both analyst and patient. Was this just about Alex's erotized primitive needs and trauma, or may it also have been, as Field (1989) suggested, that I was experiencing sadistic triumph in the face of my patient's masochism? I could not contact a part of myself that sadistically enjoyed my patient's masochism, although I did give it consideration. Perhaps the sadism and the masochism were both owned at some level by the patient himself. I knew that probably Alex had sexualized his primitive, infantile needs, and that his cravings could trigger sexual arousal in his analyst. Therefore, I understood this to be an enactment through sexual response. This is how an infantile Alex experienced early life with his mother: a way of creating a powerful impact on his analyst, allowing her to know how unconscious communication occurred between himself and his mother—excitement and frustration being paramount. For my part, Alex's cravings for me may well have excited an aspect of myself that was vulnerable to maternal erotic desire (Welles & Wrye, 1991; Wrye & Welles, 1989). Shortly after I experienced sexual arousal in a session with Alex, he began to bring his sexual and "romantic" thoughts about me to the sessions. As soon as he was able to do so, my sexual arousal experienced in the way I have described, ceased. As time went by, Alex was less consumed by desire—his for me or the wish for mine towards him. Interestingly, this then freed me to enjoy him as an adult male who was desirable and sexually attractive. However, I did not see this as an enactment. There was more erotic, less eroticized transference, and, correspondingly, a complementary erotic countertransference. Elsewhere (2004, and Chapters Four and Five), I have emphasized, in agreement with Mann (1999), my sense of the necessity of a "good enough erotic transference and countertransference".

Responses of the analyst to patients with hysterical personality

Inevitably, there are sado-masochistic elements in the sexuality of the hysteric as well as that of the borderline, but there is a marked difference in the countertransference. Britton says,

> the characteristic countertransference in the analysis of the border-line patient . . . is one of feeling constrained or tyrannised. In contrast, until the hysterical defensive organisation breaks down the analyst's feeling is of being especially important, and the risk is of an unconscious collusive partnership of mutual admiration. [1999, p. 11]

In this chapter, I have been focusing on the rescue fantasy that I feel takes hold of the analyst with these patients. If I examine Britton's statement in relation to Sam and Alex, it would certainly seem to hold true. Sam offered me continuous invitations to be aroused with him and act out sexually: they were a permanent feature of the first years of his analysis. My feelings would certainly frequently come under the heading "constrained", as with the clinical example I gave, and occasionally "tyrannized", which happened when he tried to beat me down over fees for missed sessions. Certainly "rescue" was far from my experience with Sam, although that does not mean that I could not have positive and warm feelings towards him. The exchange between us, I feel, had more to do with handling and containing his acting out (the analyst as observer) rather than addressing my enactments. However, I have suggested that being constrained and perhaps "retreating from the patient's vantage point" (Schwaber, 1992) could also be seen as an enactment.

In contrast, *rescue* has been a strong feature of my work with hysterical patients. Easser and Lesser (1965) write of the hysterics' "egocentric need to test love through interaction with others" (p. 395), thus, in my view, illustrating the basis of the "seduction" of the analyst into a rescuing enactment.

Where I was involved in an extreme countertransference fantasy with my female patient, Mary, I was also inclined to rescue her from her struggles. With my patient Lisa, and the offer of a towel, there is no question that I was drawn into rescuing a patient whose mother apparently did not do so. She had a long history of feeling misunderstood and let down. With Alex, where the enactment may have been with seductive words, albeit they were words that "touched" (Quinodoz, 2003), each time the words came as rescue from his rage and masochistic struggles. Where I have described my sexual feelings with Alex, the rescue is, perhaps, less obvious. However, it is my belief that my sexual arousal in the session did actually relieve him of his isolation in carrying the sense of guilt and negative feelings about his sexuality. I, too, had to deal with these feelings. It was often in a session following one in which I had felt sexually aroused that Alex could bring more directly his love and sexual feelings towards me. Thereupon, my body ceased to enact.

Gabbard writes on "Sexual excitement and countertransference love in the analyst" and suggests that "rescue themes are prominent in the erotic countertransference responses of both male and female analysts" (1994, p, 1098). However, this is not elaborated. My contention, which I hope to have illustrated, is that this is especially so in the case of hysterical patients.

If I return here to Britton's statement regarding the countertransference with the hysteric, and accept the notion of "mutual admiration", then this, too, would explain why an analyst would respond by wanting to rescue a patient who seems to be in trouble. It may also serve to make us wonder whether, in fact, the patient unconsciously stages "being in trouble" in order to give his/her analyst an opportunity to rescue him/her.

I feel I should not leave my thoughts on hysterical patients without mentioning, at least, the now widely held view that their theatricality is symbolic of witnessing the primal scene. Freud, in his paper, "Observations on transference-love", compared work with the hysteric to being at the theatre when "a cry of fire is raised during a theatrical performance" (1915a, p. 162). Perelberg (1999) and Britton (1999, 2003) have both written extensively about the link between hysteria and primal scene fantasies. This is not the subject of this chapter, but it is very likely that this notion has a dominant part to play in the analyst's wish to rescue.

Conclusion

Thinking though the clinical vignettes I have offered up for consideration in this chapter, I would conclude that, on the whole, they have shown that countertransference enactments have furthered understanding and contributed to the development of the patients. With Lisa and the towel, this is more debatable, but even here I do not think progress was obstructed. Indeed, it helped to further my thinking. The value of enactments, as I believe is now commonly understood, is that they are signifiers and alert the analyst to what she/he may not otherwise have understood. Self-awareness in the analyst is the key to creative and valuable outcomes of countertransference enactments. Chused said, "It is the scrutiny of the enactment, not the enactment itself, which will lead to a new understanding of the transference" (1991, p. 637). She concluded her paper, as I will conclude this chapter, with her valuable comments, "Viewed as yet another source of information, greeted with curiosity and not guilt, enactments can become part of the analytic process from which we all learn" (ibid.).

CHAPTER EIGHT

A question of absence

"By absence this good means I gain,
That I can catch her,
Where none can watch her,
In some close corner of my brain . . ."

(Hoskins, 1602)

This chapter has come about through struggles to process my countertransference, over several years, towards a female patient (Rose) who attended only rarely for her twice-weekly sessions. Her absences raised numerous questions, which I shall endeavour to examine more fully. On a regular basis, at best she would come to half of her sessions per month and at one point she came to two sessions out of a possible forty over a period of five and a half months. Payment for missed sessions during prolonged absences was very erratic, invoices sometimes accumulating for 2–3 months before payment was received. I never knew if she would arrive, telephone, or there would be a void instead of a session. At the times when either I needed to write to her, or she arrived for a session, all smiling, often very late, I was having to work hard to "tolerate my countertransference" (Carpy, 1989).

Gurevitch (2008) quotes Faimberg (2005) as saying "an absence is a presence that attacks". This is similar to O'Shaughnessy's thinking in her now seminal paper, "The absent object", wherein she specifies how initially "the absent object is a bad object which is leaving the baby to starve and die" (1964, p. 34). O'Shaughnessy goes on to stress, however, the importance of absence in development. Absence (tolerance of frustration) is essential for thought to develop and allows the growing child to know reality through thought. Eventually, with healthy growth, it becomes established that "absence is a natural and essential condition of a relationship which otherwise becomes a symbiosis detrimental to the separate identity of either person" (*ibid.*, p. 42).

However, the absences referred to above are usually short, temporary absences as opposed to the absences I am writing about here, which are not only unpredictable but often extremely prolonged. An overriding factor has been the fact that each week I have been kept "dangling in uncertainty" (Brenman Pick, 2002). In the earlier years of our relationship, Rose would not let me know when she missed a session, but over time and with some attempt at exploration, this changed, so that later on she would usually ring just before or just after her session time. I have gradually come to understand that Rose needed to convey unspeakable rage, strong affects of a sado-masochistic nature, and experiences of virtual starvation and death. These are only just bearable because *the sense of something alive is sustained through rage and hatred* (Ogden, 1995). (Rage and hatred were certainly not the only feelings I had towards Rose, and in sessions I would feel warm and empathic at times. However, these strong negative affects were often dominant during her absences.)

I have come to know all this through my countertransference over several years of "work". Work is mentioned in inverted commas because, for much of the time, the only person doing some work with the overwhelming affects was myself. Most of the time, along the way, letters from me which may have indicated that perhaps we needed to consider the future of her therapy and the possibility of bringing it to an end, were felt as totally devastating to Rose. The force of her reaction was such that I came to know how much she needed me to be here for her and tolerate her absence without retaliation (Winnicott, 1971). I came to this realization through a random thought one day relating to a Jewish joke, which goes as follows. A Jew is stranded on a desert island. He sets about building for himself two synagogues—one which he attends regularly and one which he never goes to! I needed to be here for Rose so that she could have her object waiting uncertainly for her, while in her own mind, at a conscious level, she said she was committed to her therapy and there were always arguable and cogent reasons why she did not attend. Some regular examples were: meetings at work, too busy, too upset, problems of child-care, illness, deaths, funerals, traffic jams, getting lost in her car, problems in her home life. Like the second synagogue, I came to understand that I was felt to be vital to her sense of what is needed for her survival. Thomas (2006) would seem to have reached a similar understanding when she states, "Absence from the therapy felt crucial for her [i.e., the patient's] survival".

Rose could choose to come to me or not, but *I needed to be here as a sound and solid base for her to keep that choice alive.*

Rose

Rose was referred to me by a colleague some five years before writing this chapter. She was a married woman, in her late forties, with adult children, interested in further professional development, and was attending suitable courses to that end. She struck me initially as a pleasant, mild-mannered, friendly woman, somewhat anxious, but keen and interested to begin psychotherapy.

The contract between us was for twice-weekly sessions, although she said that at some future date she may want a third session.

When I reflected on our first meeting, I realized the scene was set then for future missed sessions. Ogden (1989) in his chapter, "The initial analytic meeting", states,

> Everything that the analysand says (and does not say) in the first hours can be heard in the light of an unconscious warning to the analyst concerning the reasons why neither the analyst nor the patient should enter into this doomed and dangerous relationship. [p. 182]

In Rose's case, there was a "warning" that she suffered regularly and frequently from bronchitis, and, indeed, the second session was cancelled for just that reason.

Her personal history was that she was her parents' second child and had been relentlessly taunted by her older sister who, she later realized, was extremely jealous of her. Her mother sounds to have been critical, claustrophobically repressive, and occasionally violent towards her. She reportedly had an easier, more loving relationship with her father, felt to be kind but absent. Currently, her father was terminally ill, being cared for by mother, carers, and Rose, too, when possible. Over the past few years, both parents have died, and the consequence of each death was that Rose did not attend sessions for 2–3 months on each occasion.

She did show distress in our initial session, recalling how anxious she was between the ages of 13–16, fearing that she would die, but, with later insight, she came to know that much of this anxiety arose from repressed hostility towards both her mother and her older sister. The earlier deprivations in her life would be around the traumas of non-attunement and/or impingement, both of these leaving an infant in a state of near starvation. She added that she had always felt a failure and related it concretely to failing her 11+ examination, but could see from an interpretation I made that she failed to gain the appropriate empathic love and attention she craved from her parents and sister, but most of all from her mother.

This, in the light of Ogden's words (1989), can be seen in hindsight as a warning of the type of (m)other I was to become to Rose, at least in my countertransference: condemning, critical, punitive, and rejecting. Thinking of Sandler's thesis, too, on role responsiveness (1976), I frequently felt persecuted by Rose as my absent object/patient with whom I could not engage. In this case it was *I* who was the failure. I could not offer her an ongoing and successful therapy with mutual trust and involvement on both sides. Instead, there was erratic contact and a patient who behaved after a long absence (often without prior notification) either as if nothing unusual had happened, or, alternatively, came in to see me with a rather obsequious and apologetic manner. This could trigger in me, at times, feelings of sadistic rage towards her, which I had to monitor very carefully. By using Carpy's helpful paper (1989), I managed to forgive myself for "partial acting out". On one occasion, for example, I found myself rather sharply questioning Rose's commitment to her therapy. She was quite upset that I managed to see her as not committed when, in her own mind, she claimed to feel totally committed.

Rose's aggression was almost totally split off. Later, I came to see her as "dissociated". It came into the session through stories of both work and home life, where colleagues and/or her partner were uncaring, harsh, spiteful, and dismissive of her. People just did not understand. She had reproduced a (m)other and/or older sister in many of her outside relationships. She was often full of "grudge" (Khan, 1975) towards all those who did her down in some way, misunderstood her, and did not believe her. Of course, it was obvious to me—and to Rose to some extent—that she was reproducing these tormenting figures from her childhood, not just in her external relationships, but also in her constant concern about my critical attitude towards her. The difficulty was that this is often exactly how I did feel towards her and the temptation to "enactment" (Chapter Seven) was, at times, overwhelming.

Another way I felt enactments took place between us was over the method of payment. Initially, I had asked her to pay by cheque on receipt of the monthly account. For several months she brought cash, giving me various "reasons" why she could not pay by cheque. Often the payment was quite late, and temptation got the better of me and I accepted the cash, while trying to explore the cheque situation. After a while, I learnt that her therapy was a well-guarded secret from her husband, as was her secret other bank account in another town from where she lived. The task of paying me, therefore, was extremely complex and convoluted. She was adamant that it would be disastrous for her husband to know she was paying out money for therapy, as it would create yet another crisis in their relationship. Thus, she remained in control while I felt undermined, yet grateful to have been remunerated at last! I came to understand her payments as symbolizing a childhood set-up where little Rose felt grateful that mother was at least meeting some of her needs, although there may have been an uneasy sense of having been bribed over the transaction. The problem between us was largely that Rose did not attend regularly enough for much to be understood in this way. This is perhaps another example of my feeling that I was doing "the work" while the patient was, seemingly innocently, "trying her best to please".

One year into the therapy, Rose was able to talk to me about the "sham" she felt her marriage had been, and the telling of this was not only a relief to her but felt like something of a breakthrough, both in her trust of me and in her capacity to face reality. It allowed us to explore her masochistic part in her relationships and seemed to be, at least temporarily, a turning point in her therapy. It was the first time where she achieved almost full attendance—eight out of nine sessions. During this month she was more open with me about the things she "didn't want me to think". First, I should not think she was not committed to her therapy, and second, I should not think that she was using illness as an excuse for not coming! I did not feel strait-jacketed by these demands, but managed to retain my "freedom" to explore her fantasies around these thoughts (Symington, 1983).

This felt a short-lived but productive time in the therapy, and helped me to feel that the therapy was not a "sham" even if her marriage was.

Some months later, just prior to our second summer break, Rose, who had attended all four sessions in the preceding two weeks, had an image of being "lost in space". I spoke of how frightening this could feel, and wondered if it would help to think of my holding her in mind. She said the image had now changed to her being tied by a rope to the spaceship. She said it was a rope, much stronger than a thread would be. I played with the idea of a mother ship, and recalled her account of her own mother, who would not let her go to school on her own and insisted little Rose came home for lunch each day.

Furman (1982) wrote of the need in healthy development for mothers to be there to be left, and quoted from Anna Freud: "A mother's job is to be there to be left" (p. 15). Rose's mother seemed to carry the fear that her little daughter would get lost if she left her mother, and so it seems obvious where the fear of the other getting lost in space had originated. (See also Chapter Two on spaces in relationships.) Absences that seemed to be intolerable in childhood were being explored and faced now in the consulting room. Survival seemed to be secured by the notion of the rope, reminding me of Winnicott's games with string (1960b).

Following my theme of Chapter One, I wondered if we might begin to "travel hopefully" together. At this time I began to be hopeful that even if Rose could not recall dreams (she had told me this early on and has never brought a dream), at least there seemed to be some capacity for play between us. (It is to be hoped that, at some point, if we manage to establish an analytic process, dreams will emerge.) However, when the sessions in the autumn resumed they were again sporadic, full of grudge and a sense of persecution, mostly with rather concrete work situations.

A year after she told me about her marital situation, she again came to eight out of nine sessions in that same month. One session was movingly punctuated by a memory of her father when she was aged around three. Father had died some months prior to the telling of this. On that occasion, she recalled being excited at his coming home from work. He read her a story and hugged her, and the memory that arrived with this was Rose hiding his newspaper so she could get dad's full attention. This was poignant and led to my wish for her full attention, which maybe I could get by "hiding" all Rose's reasons and excuses for not coming to her sessions. Later, Rose came to realize, through careful challenge and interpretation on my part, that she operated in a predominantly masochistic way and slowly became able to monitor and change the way she dealt with her relationships in the external world.

During her first three years of therapy, many of the absences were accounted for because of heart and chest problems and constant bouts of infections. She not only had prolonged absences from sessions, but also from work and the courses she was taking. Gradually, however, her health improved and she had fewer absences from work. We may wonder whether her "affairs of the heart" were affected by our therapeutic relationship, but, at the same time, it is important to stress that she had an actual physical condition. However, she became stronger in asserting herself and her needs both at work and with her children, although with her husband her actions were conducted more in passive–aggressive mode (e.g., the secret bank account).

As her absences continued to be a feature, however, I did speak with her at one point about her possible fears of intimacy and involvement with me. She immediately denied a fear of intimacy and cited several close friendships. Nevertheless, my thinking took me to Khan's paper, "Dread of surrender to resourceless dependence in the analytic situation" (1972), and I think that although his case example was very different, his conclusion about a child who "had been cheated of her aggressive potential and its articulation by too good an adaptation to a part of her needs as an infant and child" holds very true for Rose. In other words, her dependency needs were met by a possessive and clinging mother, although her needs for separation and absence were not met, and so there was dread and repression of the ensuing rage this would have triggered. I think these feelings were masked by the constantly missed sessions.

And so the work progressed by increments, but frequently seemed to regress whenever another prolonged absence arose. At one point, I was taken aback when I realized how repetitive my letters had become. For instance, a letter I wrote just before the Christmas break, referring to the build-up of a debt over several months and a long period of non-attendance, requiring an urgent review of the situation and containing a "threat" not to keep the sessions open after the end of January, was mirrored almost word for word in a letter written in December three years earlier. During the interim, there had also been three similar letters.

I must emphasize that these had been written with due consideration and consultation. As I said earlier, all these ultimatums from me resulted in anger and shock from Rose and generally a return to therapy and payment of the outstanding debts. My letters felt to her as if they threatened her survival, after her absence threatened the survival of her therapy. Unfortunately, this seemed to be the currency between us much of the time.

Subsequently, there was a noticeable change in the atmosphere. Rose moved to a new job where she carried more responsibility and did not feel persecuted or criticized by her colleagues. Alongside this, I started feeling less angry, less undermined, and more able to interpret from a thinking place inside me when she did arrive for sessions.

Among all the rage and frustration in her absences, I frequently felt empathic towards Rose during our sessions together.

On her return after that Christmas (following my letter giving an ultimatum and the period of non-attendance I referred to earlier—only two sessions attended out of a possible forty), there seemed to be more of a reflective space in sessions. After letting me know of further illness and investigations, although a feared diagnosis was a false alarm, she talked to me yet again of how hurt, angry, and cheated she felt in her marriage. She had also been moved by an old photograph taken prior to her marriage; she liked the person she saw there—slimmer, happier, and much less persecuted. That made her feel angry about the life she had now. I could then speak with her about how, here with me, she had re-established a type of relationship where there is little apparent connection (Bion, 1959), so that one of us quite frequently turned to thinking about terminating it. I spoke to her, in what I felt was a gentle and non-persecutory way, of the anger that is generated in this type of relationship. I said that I could see more clearly how she needed, unconsciously, to push me to the brink to see whether I could accept living alone with that degree of rage. I also suggested that this was the only way she had known how to convey to me, not only the relationship she had now in her marriage, but the depth of the degree to which she felt alone and unconnected to her mother, her sister, and, to a lesser extent, her father. Rose seemed grateful for this insight, which, she felt, resonated deeply inside her. I felt moved and loving (see Chapter Four) in the connection we shared at that moment. I believe I had managed to speak to her in this instance in what Gurevich (2008) has called "the language of absence". She says,

> It is the task of the analyst to "address" the dissociated part directly, in the "language of absence". It will be revived only if it is alive for the analyst. Otherwise it stays absent. The notion of "absence" helps us focus our understanding of the dissociative condition as a synchronicity of the action of the other, of the psychic action, and of the intrapsychic state of affairs. [p. 566]

Discussion

The familiar saying "Absence makes the heart grow fonder" (Bayly, 1797–1839) suggests that the time spent apart leads you to care for a person even more. However, what has been so striking about Rose's absence is how it has formed a "bad presence" in my mind.

There is nothing empty about the absence, but, on the contrary, something very full. Perelberg (2003) wrote about full and empty spaces in the analytic process. She was referring to patients who attend their sessions, but she distinguished between those who leave an "empty space in the analyst's mind . . . a dryness . . . a kind of depressive feeling" and those who "fill the consulting room . . . the analyst feels consistently involved in the patient's analysis" (p. 579). Here, with Rose, she was technically absent but I felt powerfully involved with what Perelberg would call "the analyst's passion". My powerful countertransference feelings became inflamed correspondingly to the increasing number of cancelled sessions. After what sometimes felt like a breakthrough (Field, 1996), followed by prolonged absence, I was often left with an almost murderous rage—in fantasy at varying times wanting to cry with frustration, destroy something or someone, shout at the patient, or sadistically cut her off. Whatever I felt, it was never either "dry" or "depressed". I think that I sometimes felt quite crazy (Searles, 1959b) with these strong affects—after all it was just another cancellation—but later the relief of being able to process my responses as fragments of my patient's mind in her family of origin could rescue my sanity. What I experienced, at times, is described here by de Urtubey: "When the setting is breached by the absent patient, the analyst finds himself confronted with his own psychotic part that has been set free, sometimes accompanied by the psychotic part projected by the patient" (1995, p. 691).

In Bion's words, my patient made constant "attacks on linking" (1959) through her absences—a destructive attack on a mother who could not contain her infant's projective processes. I felt I was being constantly tested as to whether or not I could do so, and, under-standably, sometimes I failed. I frequently became the therapist who could not be involved, connected, or able to cure.

The expectations of continuity, availability, and contact, con-stantly thwarted by the frustrations of absence, solitude, and dis-continuity were, I felt, the scenarios of Rose's bleak childhood. There was no available object to understand and tolerate her rage and frustration, so she became compliant and dissociated. Gurevich (2008) describes the essential difference between splitting and dissociation. Splitting, she says, is horizontal and occurs between conscious and unconscious, while dissociation is vertical and occurs in consciousness (p. 565). Early traumatic wounds lead to dissociated and disrupted selves where "self-states are shed in order to keep this 'association' intact, to hold in place the connection, the bond, with the other" (p. 564).

During sessions, I was rarely, if ever, in touch with the degree of rage or passion that I was in contact with during Rose's absences. I came to see later how these absences had to generate such feelings in me, leading to my knowing more deeply about her dissociated state of mind.

I recall here Sabbadini's paper, "Listening to silence" (1991). As he says, "behind all silence there is an unconscious fantasy which the silence—like the dream or the symptom—both conceals and expresses at the same time" (p. 409). In this case, I would say, for "silence" read "absence". Just as Sabbadini writes of the silence as a message that there is something the patient cannot say, so I read the absence as a message indicating that Rose needed to have a psychotherapist she could not come to see. How else could I know of the lonely, mad place Rose had inhabited in the past, and, to an extent, still continued to inhabit.

Winston (2009) wrote of absence, linking it to anorexia nervosa. As such, Rose was not anorexic, but she certainly treated her therapy in an anorexic way, mainly having little "tastes" that rarely nourished at irregular intervals. I seemed to be the mother who could not tempt her with a feed, while, to ponder on this in reverse, I was the starving child whose mother rarely came to feed me or hold me. Winston also mentioned the absence of aggression, which becomes "transformed into 'masochistic passivity and self-denial', which both conceal and express the aggression" (p. 79). He illustrated how the masochism and sadism in the patient serve to attack the analyst's attempts to make contact, so that the analyst has little satisfaction in having been of help. He also somewhat described my patient in referring to an impoverished fantasy life where dreams are absent. Winston writes of the deadness in the therapeutic interaction, which I recognized on occasions in my sessions with Rose. (In Rose's absences, as I have described, my countertransference was mostly alive and passionate.) At times, in our sessions, I would find myself in a place that felt empty or like "a dead space" (Wrye, 1993). "Deadspace" is described by Wrye as a genderless area where many severely disturbed patients reside. It is worth noting here that she sees this as a result of "early unreliable contact whether it takes the form of excessive unpredictability, suffocating overinvolvement, or maternal absence" (p. 244). "Unreliable contact" is the stuff that has coloured our relationship from the start. Mann refers to the "deadspace" as reflective of a patient lacking "erotic vitality" (2001, p. 72), and, for quite some time, this would accord with my experience of Rose. These issues are also addressed in Chapters Four, Five, and Six.

I have slowly reached the understanding that Rose's absences were necessary for me to know that she carried deep in her psyche something almost intolerable and yet it was vital that it become tolerated. It is possible, though not yet fully understood or metabolized by me, that the deadness within some sessions was followed by a subsequent absence and, thereby, the reoccurrence of rage. This, in turn, leads to some idea of a relationship that, albeit somewhat perverse, is one that is very much alive.

It has been my task, with this understanding, to bring the absence into the room. This is essential because the sado-masochistic overlay to our relationship could not be tolerated indefinitely. Gurevich (2008) stresses the need to re-experience within an attuned relationship both the traumatic experience and the dissociated reactions to it, so that "it is rendered with meaning, symbolization and validation, and enables the survival mode of dissociation to be relinquished" (p. 561).

This is reminiscent of Winnicott's paper, "Fear of breakdown" (1974), where the original breakdown, which is not conscious, has to be re-experienced within the analytic relationship.

Perhaps it could be reasonably argued that when Rose did not come for her sessions for months at a time, coupled with her non-payment of invoices, which then led to my actions of letter writing and ultimatums, that there was a serious "breakdown" in analytic holding. Absences, by then, had continued almost beyond my endurance, and so I was the one to react to this repetition of a childhood scenario. As Thomas says in her paper, "absence and absent-mindedness", "survival of the deadliness and despair that absent patients may evoke in their therapist is regarded as a key factor in the work" (2006). To the extent that the letter writing and its contents were "jointly created by therapist and patient" (Chapter Seven), it was an "enactment", but it is difficult to imagine how else things could have been managed. However, what then ensued was Rose's return to therapy for a while, her reconnection with me, and some further understanding within our re-established relationship. The "breakdown" was temporarily repaired.

Concern about enactments led me to regular consultation, where the fraught issue of indebtedness was stressed. In addition, we focused on the hatred that, with her prolonged absences, becomes very alive—certainly in me, but probably in Rose too, albeit unconscious. Thomas (2006), too, stressed the necessity of consultation when working with absent patients, bearing in mind the sense of meaninglessnes they can generate. An enormous effort is invested in "making something out of nothing".

Money-Kyrle (1971) cites the importance of three separate life tasks: "the recognition of the breast as a supremely good object, the recognition of the parents' intercourse as a supremely creative act, and the recognition of the inevitability of time and ultimately death" (p. 103). These tasks, if accomplished, give life meaning. In Rose's case, she would appear to have been overwhelmed with fantasies and fears of death as a young woman, and later these were accentuated by some of her very real physical symptoms. I had not yet become the good object/mother who could be established inside her, allowing her to enjoy and rely on me (and then ultimately to mourn that she could not have me forever). That would, in developmental terms, then allow her to move into the recognition of the creativity of the parental intercourse. Sadly for Rose, her inner world has been largely empty of this fantasy and experience.

Conclusion

I think we have, tentatively, begun to touch on the meaning(s) of Rose's not coming to her sessions and not allowing herself a continuity of contact with her therapist. The idea is consolidating that together we were repeating an irresolvable trauma. By a thread, with Rose's help, I managed to hold on to the internal setting. Her hatred of, and disappointment in, her primary object almost succeeded (unconsciously) in destroying that setting, but it would seem that Rose's determination to survive has so far won the day, in spite of wishes for, and terrors of, death, in relation to both herself and her objects. More consciously, she would have been in touch with a sense of helplessness, but hatred and a fear of annihilation have not been not far behind.

Green (1997) has defined absence as something or someone not present, creating "a representation of the absence of representation, which expresses itself as a void, emptiness, futility or meaninglessness. . . . an absent negative bond" (p. 1074). Bergmann (2000) calls this a parental "not-thereness", and suggests that an illusory state can develop following adolescence (Rose's fantasies that she was going to die). Bergmann suggests that "the perverse enactment erases the 'not-thereness' by a fantasy or enactment" (p. 41).

Rose's "perverse" ways of trying to manage her helplessness and her consequent rage over her early traumas were in her prolonged absences. These were an attempt to triumph over her object and reverse the set-up so that she became the one who behaved in such a way towards her object, whereby she may have gained masochistic pleasure. Her principal objects in her external world were her mother, her older sister, and her husband, all of whom were felt to be sadistic, while her father was weak and largely unavailable. These are the props for the theatre of sado-masochistic object relating so powerfully played out in the analytic process.

However, I believe that Rose was also very frightened. As Winnicott (1963) said, "It is joy to be hidden and disaster not to be found" (p. 186). What would it mean for her to come to life, be found by me, and for us to find meaning? Rose may have felt herself to be between a rock and a hard place. She would have to mourn all that she did not have and to discover and own a deadened part of herself.

Rose held tenaciously to her therapy when she had an experience of my attempts to end it. This, in itself, gave me hope that there might come a time when we could have a relationship where her absences and my frustration would cease to be the currency between us. I hoped that she would allow me to penetrate her defences and, through use of my countertransference, reach out to her dissociated state wherein her fear and sadism lie. Thereafter, if she could allow true mourning for what she did not have, then she would no longer need to avoid or seek revenge on the objects who have so chronically deprived her and let her down. Gurevich wrote of love expressed through a "language of tenderness" that she sees as vital between mother and infant. This allows for the spontaneous development of the self. If Rose remains overwhelmed by her fear of her unavailable and sadistic objects, then, however, it is likely that we would not be able to resolve her continued absences from our sessions.

I cannot "know", I can only wait and see . . . and, as T. S. Eliot says in East Coker,

> I said to my soul, be still, and wait without hope
> For hope would be hope for the wrong thing; wait without love,
> For love would be love of the wrong thing; there is yet faith
> But the faith and the love and the hope are all in the waiting.

CHAPTER NINE

Dilemmas of a psychotherapist

That our profession is fraught with dilemmas was brought home to me by my introduction to the London Centre for Psychotherapy in 1978, when I was interviewed by the Director, Dr Ilse Seglow, for a place on the qualifying course. I was a few minutes early, and she showed me into a room where 8–10 identical chairs were arranged in a circle.

She asked me to sit down, saying she would be with me shortly. When Dr Seglow entered the room, she said, "Aha, I wonder why you have chosen to sit in my chair!" Thus began my new life as a trainee, and subsequently a qualified psychotherapist, where dilemmas for both patient and therapist are a constant in the work. In one way, there being no absolute rights and wrongs is very freeing (apart from gross boundary violations, of course), but in another way the task of analysis means there are constant dilemmas to be explored and worked with. Hence the title of this book: *The Impossibility of Knowing*.

Dilemmas regarding action

What do a budgerigar and a spider have in common? This is not an idle riddle, but comes from two completely different situations within the analysis of two female patients, both presenting me with dilemmas where I had little time to think.

First, the budgerigar. Jane, a patient who had been in twice-weekly therapy for some time, rang the doorbell on time for her session. She looked at me and then looked down to the ground.

Standing at her feet was a budgerigar. She asked me what I thought we should do. I was taken aback and confused, and then retreated to my analytic stance, which was to suggest that as it was now her session time I thought she should come in and we could begin her session. I cannot now recall the substance of that particular session, although much of Jane's material had been around the experience of not having had a good enough mother and the transference was punctuated by idealization and denigration. After our session had ended, I went out into the front garden and found a mass of budgerigar feathers on the lawn. I do not know if Jane noticed these or not—the subject was never raised again—but I was left feeling as if I had murdered a little, helpless, domestic bird.

In hindsight, would there have been a "right" thing to do? Should Jane and I have tried to catch the bird in a box that I would have to search for within my home? If we had done so, which of us would then have taken it to the local vet? Should we have started the session on the doorstep and discussed various options of what to do with the budgerigar? Nothing would have seemed the right thing to do, I believe.

My second example regarding dilemmas of action is to do with a spider. Lisa, who was in five-times-weekly analysis with me (see also Chapter Seven) was quite phobic about spiders. One day, while she was lying on the couch, a spider started to walk across the ceiling right above her. She became rigid and turned white, and asked whether I could help. I asked quite quickly what she wanted, and she said something about just getting rid of it. Again, here, I had little time to think. She got up off the couch and I stood on the couch and used a tissue to trap the spider, but I also killed it.

She was horrified. She was a person who loved animals and spent much time retrieving birds and mice from the claws of her cat. In my haste for action, to do something and to rescue Lisa, I feel I had not only killed the spider, but somehow killed her vision of me for quite some time as a therapist who can be kind and compassionate. Again, here, my hasty action to try to resolve a dilemma ended with my feeling that I had committed a murder. It would almost certainly have been better had I trapped the spider in a tissue and then opened the window and put it outside. Perhaps I should have done nothing at all, but put the dilemma back to Lisa, as I think I should have done with Jane, too (although it would have been much harder, taking place on the doorstep).

Margaret comes into the session on a very hot day, having made strenuous efforts to get to me on time, obviously very hot and thirsty. She is palpably uncomfortable and in need of water, though does not request it.

The dilemma is—do I leave the room to get her a glass of water (an enactment), or do I leave her feeling hot, sticky, and uncomfortable and work with it? What does a therapist do who wants to keep the frame secure but feels sympathetic on a human level to the plight of the patient? Of course, we can talk about why she puts herself in this situation. I could have left a glass in the bathroom so she could get her own water (but I had not done so); so again my dilemma about action or no action led to a decision that resulted in an enactment, as described in Chapter Seven.

In all these examples, to act or not to act does, I think, result in some kind of enactment on the part of the analyst, as there will be times when "abstinence" becomes more of a sadistic withholding. I actually did not "know" how best to proceed in any of these instances.

Dilemmas regarding finances

We may all have had dilemmas about charging patients in certain circumstances. Some charge for missed sessions come what may, others charge half fee or waive fees for transport strikes, heavy snow, funerals, sudden illness, prolonged illness, hospital admissions, deaths, and weddings. Recently, in discussion with colleagues, it was suggested to me that to do anything other than charge for a missed session was to play God. This may be so, and naturally makes the task much easier for me if I charge for every missed session, whatever the reason. Perhaps it allows the patient to be angry with me as his/her "greedy" therapist? This decision would also, of course, remove any of my own dilemmas about charging.

What, then, when patients (luckily there are few) choose not to pay for their sessions, and month follows month with non-payment, many excuses, procrastination, bounced cheques, etc? (See also Chapter Eight.) At what point do I terminate the treatment and then, if I do, in what way do I pursue the money owing? There are solicitors, small claims courts, debt collectors. All these present us with choices, dilemmas, and difficulties in holding to our analytic ways of working.

Dilemmas regarding publication of clinical material

As Gabbard (2000) stressed so clearly in his paper, "Disguise or consent", the issue of publication gives the author a cluster of dilemmas to deal with, the most complex, in my opinion (as someone who has published quite frequently), being the attempt to gain "consent".

Many analysts do not write or publish: this is their choice. Some of us find that writing, at times, allows for exploration and working through of issues that become close to our hearts.

We publish in the hope that what we have to say will be helpful and of interest to others, but of course, inevitably, there must be some form of narcissistic element to the publishing as well.

So, herein lies another dilemma: do we abstain from publishing because it may be prove to be harmful to the patient, thereby also denying ourselves a degree of gratification? Or do we grasp a nettle if writing and publishing adds to the satisfaction of our work and is part of what we do?

This chapter, and, indeed, this book, offers no answers. In our daily work there are usually no absolute rights or wrongs but the continuous struggle with dilemmas, such as the one wherein I began my own analytic journey. Which stance shall I take at this moment? Which chair shall I sit in? Ideally, it will, above all, be my own chair, and I will be able to lay claim to it. It is not a chair of knowledge, but one of thinking, being, and sensing; one in which I sit continually prepared to struggle with the everyday dilemmas of psychoanalytic work.

REFERENCES

Armstrong-Perlman, E. (1991). The allure of the bad object. *Free Associations, 3*(23): 343–356.

Bacal, H. A. (1987). British object-relations theorists and self psychology: some critical reflections. *International Journal of Psychoanalysis, 68*: 87–98.

Baker, R. (1993). The patient's discovery of the psychoanalyst as a new object. *International Journal of Psychoanalysis, 74*: 1223–1233.

Balint, A. (1949). Love for the mother and mother-love. *International Journal of Psychoanalysis, 30*: 251–259.

Balint, M. (1955). Friendly expanses—horrid empty spaces. *International Journal of Psychoanalysis, 36*: 225–241.

Balint, M. (1959). *Thrills and Regressions*. London: Maresfield Library, 1987.

Balint, M. (1968). *The Basic Fault*. London: Tavistock.

Barratt, B. (1994). Critical notes on the psychoanalyst's theorizing. *Journal of the American Psychoanalytic Association, 42*: 697–725.

Bateman, A. (1998). Thick- and thin-skinned organisations and enactment in borderline and narcissistic disorders. *International Journal of Psychoanalysis, 79*: 13–25.

Bayly, T. H. (1797–1839). *Isle of Beauty*. Cited in: *The Oxford Dictionary of Quotations* (p. 36). Oxford: Oxford University Press, 1953.

Bell, D. (1992). Hysteria—a contemporary Kleinian perspective. *British Journal of Psychotherapy, 9*: 169–180.

Benjamin, J. (2001). The primal leap of psychoanalysis, from body to speech: Freud, feminism, and the vicissitudes of transference. In: M. Dimen & A. Harris (Eds.), *Storms in Her Head* (pp. 31–54). New York: Other Press.

Bergmann, M. (2000). A world of illusion: the creation of a perverse solution as a reaction to parental emotional absence. *Canadian Journal of Psychoanalysis, 8*: 41–66.

Bick, E. (1968). The experience of the skin in early object-relations. In: *Melanie Klein Today, Mostly Theory*. London: Routledge, 1988.

Billow, R. (1999). An intersubjective approach to entitlement. *Psychoanalytic Quarterly, 68*: 441–461.

Bion, W. (1959). Attacks on linking. *International Journal of Psychoanalysis, 40*: 308–315.

Blass, R. B., & Simon, B. (1994). The value of the historical perspective to contemporary psychoanalysis: Freud's seduction hypothesis. *International Journal of Psychoanalysis, 77*: 677–693.

Blechner, M. (1987). Entitlement and narcissism: paradise sought. *Contemporary Psychoanalysis, 23*: 244–255.

Blum, H. P. (1996). Seduction trauma: representation, deferred action, and pathogenic development. *Journal of the American Psychoanalytic Association., 44*: 1147–1164.

Boesky, D. (1982). Acting out: a reconsideration of the concept. *International Journal of Psychoanalysis, 63*: 39–55.

Bollas, C. (1987a). Loving hate. In: *The Shadow of the Object*. London: Free Association Books.

Bollas, C. (1987b). *The Shadow of the Object: Psychoanalysis of the Unthought Known*. London: Free Association Books.

Bollas, C. (2000). *Hysteria*. London: Routledge.

Bott Spillius, E. (1993). Varieties of envious experience. *International Journal of Psychoanalysis, 74*: 1199–1212.

Brenman, E. (1985a). Cruelty and narrowmindedness. *International Journal of Psychoanalysis, 66*: 273–281.

Brenman, E. (1985b). Hysteria. *International Journal of Psychoanalysis, 66*: 423–432.

Brenman Pick, I. (2002). Dangling in uncertainty. Unpublished paper presented to Melanie Klein Conference London, June.

Britton, R. (1989). The missing link. In: R. Britton, E. O'Shaughnessy, M. Feldman, & J. Steiner (Eds.), *The Oedipus Complex Today: Clinical Implications* (pp. 83–101). London: Karnac.

Britton, R. (1998). *Belief and Imagination*. London: Routledge.

Britton, R. (1999). Getting in on the act: the hysterical solution. *International Journal of Psychoanalysis, 80*: 1–14.

Britton, R. (2003). *Sex, Death and the Superego*. London: Karnac.

Bromberg, P. M. (1983). The mirror and the mask: on narcissism and psychoanalytic growth. *Contemporary Psychoanalysis, 19*: 359–387.

Caper, R. (1998). Panel discussion on "Seduction": chaired by Sandor Abend. *International Journal of Psychoanalysis, 79*: 168–170.

Carpy, D. (1989). Tolerating the countertransference: a mutative process. *International Journal of Psychoanalysis, 70*: 287–294.

Charles, M. (1997). Betrayal. *Contemporary Psychoanalysis, 33*: 109–122.

Chodoff, P. (1978). Psychotherapy of the hysterical personality disorder. *Journal of the American Academy of Psychoanalysis, 6*: 497–510.

Chused, J. F. (1991). The evocative power of enactments. *Journal of the American Psychoanalytic Association, 39*: 615–639.

Coltart, N. (1986). Slouching towards Bethlehem. In: *Slouching Towards Bethlehem and Further Psychoanalytic Explorations* (pp. 1–14). London: Free Assocation Books, 1992.

Coltart, N. (1992a). *Slouching Towards Bethlehem and Further Psychoanalytic Explorations*. London: Free Association Books.

Coltart, N. (1992b). What does it mean: "Love is not enough"? In: *Slouching Towards Bethlehem and Further Psychoanalytic Explorations* (pp. 111–127). London: Free Association Books.

Coltart, N. (1993). *How to Survive as a Psychotherapist*. London: Sheldon Press.

Darwin, C. (1859). *On the Origin of Species*. London: John Murray.

Davies, J. M. (1994). Love in the afternoon: a relational reconsideration of desire and dread in the countertransference. *Psychoanalytic Dialogues, 4*: 153–170.

Davies, J. M. (1998a). Between the disclosure and foreclosure of erotic transference–countertransference. *Psychoanalytic Dialogues, 8*: 747–766.

Davies, J. M. (1998b). Thoughts on the nature of desires: the ambiguous, the transitional, and the poetic: reply to commentaries. *Psychoanalytic Dialogues, 8*: 805–823.

Davies, J. M. (2003). Falling in love with love: oedipal and postoedipal manifestation of idealization, mourning and erotic masochism. *Psychoanalytic Dialogues, 13*: 1–27.

Davies, J. M., & Frawley, M. G. (1992). Dissociative processes and transference–countertransference paradigms in the psychoanalytically oriented treatment of adult survivors of childhood sexual abuse. *Psychoanalytic Dialogues, 2*: 5–36.

De Urtubey, L. (1995). Countertransference effects of absence. *International Journal of Psychoanalysis, 76*: 683–694.

Easser, B. R., & Lesser, S. R. (1965). Hysterical personality: a re-evaluation. *Psychoanalytic Quarterly, 34*: 390–405.

Eissler, K. R. (1993). Comments on erroneous interpretations of Freud's seduction theory. *Journal of the American Psychoanalytic Association, 41*: 571–583.

Eliot, T. S. (1935). Little Gidding. In: *Four Quartets*. London: Faber and Faber, 1949.

Eliot, T. S. (1935–1942). East Coker, no. 2 of *Four Quartets*. London: Faber and Faber, 1949.

Faimberg, H. (2005). Apres-coup. Response. *International Journal of Psychoanalysis, 86*(1): 1–6.

Fenichel, O. (1945). *The Psychoanalytic Theory of Neuroses*. New York: Norton.

Ferenczi, S. (1933). Confusion of tongues between adults and the child. In: *Final Contributions to Problems and Methods of Psycho-Analysis*. London: Hogarth Press, 1955.

Field, N. (1989). Listening with the body. *British Journal of Psychotherapy, 5*: 512–522.

Field, N. (1996). *Breakdown and Breakthrough*. London: Routledge.

Frayn, D. H. (1993). The influence of dyadic factors on enactments and other regressive forms of acting out. *Canadian Journal of Psychoanalysis, 1*(2): 61–83.

Freud, S. (1905d). *Three Essays on the Theory of Sexuality. S.E., 7*: 125–245. London: Hogarth.

Freud, S. (1906). Letter to Jung, quoted in Bettelheim, B. (1983). *Freud and Man's Soul*. New York: Alfred Knopf Inc.

Freud, S. (1909d). *Notes Upon a Case of Obsessional Neurosis. S.E., 10*: 153–249. London: Hogarth.

Freud, S. (1910h). A special type of choice of object made by men (contributions to the psychology of love). *S.E., 11*: 163–176. London: Hogarth.

Freud, S. (1912–1913). *Totem and Taboo. S.E., 13*: 1–161. London: Hogarth.

Freud, S. (1914c). *On Narcissism: An Introduction. S.E., 14*: 73–102. London: Hogarth.

Freud, S. (1915a). Observations on transference-love. *S.E., 12*: 157–171. London: Hogarth.

Freud, S. (1916d). Some character-types met with in psycho-analytic work. *S.E., 14*: 309–336. London Hogarth.

Freud, S. (1917e). Mourning and melancholia. *S.E., 14*: 243–258. London: Hogarth.

Freud, S. (1920g). *Beyond the Pleasure Principle. S.E., 18*: 7–64. London: Hogarth.

Freud, S. (1923b). *The Ego and the Id. S.E., 19*: 3–66. London: Hogarth.

Freud, S. (1930a). *Civilization and its Discontents. S.E., 21*: 59–145. London: Hogarth.

Freud, S. (1931b). Female sexuality. *S.E., 13*: 255–244. London: Hogarth.

Fromm, E. (1976). *The Art of Loving*. London: Unwin Paperbacks.

Furman, E. (1982). Mothers have to be there to be left. *Psychoanalytic Study of the Child, 37*: 15–28.

Gabbard, G. (1991). Technical approaches to transference hate in the analysis of borderline patients. *International Journal of Psychoanalysis, 72*: 625–637.

Gabbard, G. (1994). Sexual excitement and countertransference love in the analyst. *Journal of the American Psychoanalytic Association, 42*: 1083–1106.

Gabbard, G. (1996). The analyst's contribution to the erotic transference. *Contemporary Psychoanalysis, 32*: 249–272.

Gabbard, G. (2000). Disguise or consent. *International Journal of Psychoanalysis, 81*: 1071–1086.

Gabbard, G. (2003). Miscarriages of psychoanalytic treatment with suicidal patients. *International Journal of Psychoanalysis, 84*: 249–261.

Gabbard, G., & Lester, E. (1995). *Boundaries and Boundary Violations in Psychoanalysis*. New York: Basic Books.

Garcia, E. (1987). Freud's seduction theory. *Psychoanalytic Study of the Child, 42*: 443–468.

Gerrard, J. (1990). Use and abuse in psychotherapy. *British Journal of Psychotherapy, 7*: 121–128.

Gerrard, J. (2000). Ocnophilia and the interpretation of transference. *British Journal of Psychotherapy, 16*: 400–411.

Gerrard, J. (2004). Surviving Oedipus (unpublished paper presented to London Centre for Psychotherapy and Lincoln Centre).

Gerrard, J. (2007). Enactments in the countertransference: with special reference to rescue fantasies with hysterical patients. *British Journal of Psychotherapy, 23*: 217–230.

Gibran, K. (1926). On marriage. In: *The Prophet*. London: Heinemann.

Giovacchini, P. (1993). Absolute and not quite absolute dependence. In: D. Goldman (Ed.), *In One's Bones* (pp. 241–256). New York: Jason Aronson.

Gottlieb, S. (1994). Hateful relationships. *British Journal of Psychotherapy, 11*(1): 8–19.

Green, A. (1997). The intuition of the negative in playing and reality. *International Journal of Psychoanalysis, 78*: 1071–84.

Greenberg, J. (2001). The ambiguity of seduction in the development of Freud's thinking. *Contemporary Psychoanalysis, 37*: 417–426.

Grey, A. (1987). Entitlement: an interactional defense of self esteem. *Contemporary Psychoanalysis, 23*: 255–263.

Grotstein, J. S. (1990). Review of attitudes of entitlement: theoretical and clinical issues. *Psychoanalytic Books, 1*: 58–63.

Guntrip, H. (1977). *Schizoid Phenomena, Object Relations and the Self.* London: Hogarth Press.

Gurevich, H. (2008). The language of absence. *International Journal of Psychoanalysis, 89*: 561–578.

Halberstadt-Freud, H. (1996). Studies on hysteria one hundred years on: a century of psychoanalysis. *International Journal of Psychoanalysis, 77*: 983–996.

Hoffman, I. (1983). The patient as interpreter of the analyst's experience. *Contemporary Psychoanalysis, 19*: 389–422.

Hoffman, I. Z. (1998). Poetic transformations of erotic experience: commentary on paper by Jody Messler Davies. *Psychoanalytic Dialogues, 8*: 791–804.

Hoskins, J. (1602). Absence. In: F. Davison (Ed.), *A Poetical Rhapsody.* London: G. Bell, 1891.

Hughes, T. (1857). *Tom Brown's Schooldays.* London: Macmillan.

Jacobs, T. J. (1986). On countertransference enactments. *Journal of the American Psychoanalytic Association, 34*: 289–307.

Jacobson, E. (1959). The "exceptions": an elaboration of Freud's character study. *Psychoanalytic Study of the Child, 14*: 134–154.

Josephs, L. (2001). The seductive superego: the trauma of self-betrayal. *International Journal of Psychoanalysis, 82*: 701–712.

Josephs, L. (2006). The impulse to infidelity and oedipal splitting. *International Journal of Psychoanalysis, 87*: 423–437.

Kernberg, O. (1975). *Borderline Conditions and Pathological Narcissism.* New York: Jason Aronson.

Kernberg, O. (1995). *Love Relations.* New Haven, CT: Yale University Press.

Khan, M. (1972). Dread of surrender to resourceless dependence in the analytic situation. *International Journal of Psychoanalysis, 53*: 225–230.

Khan, M. (1975). Grudge and the hysteric. In: *Hidden Selves: Between Theory and Practice in Psychoanalysis* (pp. 51–58). London: Hogarth, 1983.

King, P. (1978). The affective response of the analyst to the patient's communications. In: *Time Present and Time Past*. London: Karnac, 2005.

Klein, J. (1990). Patients who are not ready for interpretations. In: *Doubts and Certainties in the Practice of Psychotherapy*. London: Karnac, 1995.

Klein, M. (1930). The importance of symbol formation in the development of the ego. *International Journal of Psychoanalysis, 11*: 24–39.

Klein, M. (1937). Love, guilt and reparation. In: M. Klein & J. Riviere (Eds.), *Love, Hate and Reparation* (pp. 57–119). New York: Norton Library, 1964.

Kohut, H. (1966). Forms and transformations of narcissism. *Journal of the American Psychoanalytic Association, 14*: 243–272.

Laplanche, J. (1995). Seduction, persecution, revelation. *International Journal of Psychoanalysis, 76*: 663–682.

Laplanche, J. (1997). The theory of seduction and the problem of the Other. *International Journal of Psychoanalysis, 78*: 653–666.

Levenson, E. A. (2006). Response to John Steiner. *International Journal of Psychoanalysis, 87*: 321–324.

Likierman, M. (1993). Primitive object love in Melanie Klein's thinking; early theoretical influences. *International Journal of Psychoanalysis, 74*: 241–253.

Lionells, M. (1986). A reevaluation of hysterical relatedness. *Contemporary Psychoanalysis, 22*: 570–597.

Loewald, H. (1979). The waning of the Oedipus complex. In: *Papers on Psychoanalysis* (pp. 384–404). New Haven, CT: Yale University Press.

Lubbe, T. (2003). Diagnosing a male hysteric: Don Juan type. *International Journal of Psychoanalysis, 84*: 1043–1059.

Main, T. F. (1957). The ailment. *British Journal of Medical Psychology, 30*: 129–145.

Mann, D. (1999). *Erotic Transference and Countertransference: Clinical Practice in Psychotherapy*. London: Routledge.

Mann, D. (2001). Erotics and ethics: the passionate dilemmas of the therapeutic couple. In: F. P. Barnes & L. Murdin (Eds.), *Values & Ethics in the Practice of Psychotherapy and Counselling* (pp. 63–81). Oxford: Oxford University Press.

McDougall, J. (1974). The psychosoma and the psychoanalytic process. *International Review of Psycho-Analysis, 1*: 437–459.

McLaughlin, J. T. (1991). Clinical and theoretical aspects of enactment. *Journal of the American Psychoanalytic Association, 39*: 595–614.

Miller, A. (1983). *The Drama of the Gifted Child and the Search for the True Self*. London: Faber and Faber.

Mitchell, J. (2000). *Mad Men and Medusas*. London: Penguin.

Mollon, P. (1993). *The Fragile Self: The Structure of Narcissistic Disturbance*. London: Whurr.

Money-Kyrle, R. (1971). The aim of psychoanalysis. *International Journal of Psychoanalysis, 52*: 103–106.

Morrison, A. P. (1986). *Essential Papers on Narcissism*. New York: New York University Press.

Moses, R., & Moses-Hrushovski, R. (1990). Reflections on the sense of entitlement. *Psychoanalytic Study of the Child, 45*: 61–78.

Norrington, S. (1996). Hate in the countertransference. Unpublished paper, presented to London Centre for Psychotherapy.

Ogden, T. (1985). On potential space. *International Journal of Psychoanalysis, 66*: 129–141.

Ogden, T. (1989). The initial analytic meeting. In: *The Primitive Edge of Experience* (pp. 169–194). New York: Jason Aronson.

Ogden, T. (1995). Analysing forms of aliveness and deadness of the transference-countertransference. *International Journal of Psychoanalysis, 76*: 695–709.

Ogden, T. H. (1996). The perverse subject of analysis. *Journal of the American Psychoanalytic Association, 44*: 1121–1146.

O'Shaughnessy, E. (1964). The absent object. *Journal of Child Psychotherapy, 11*: 34–43.

Parsons, M. (2000). *The Dove that Returns, The Dove that Vanishes*. London: Routledge.

Perelberg, R. J. (1999). The interplay of identifications: violence, hysteria and the repudiation of femininity. In: G. Kohon (Ed.), *The Dead Mother—The Work of André Green* (pp. 173–192). London: Routledge.

Perelberg, R. J. (2003). Full and empty spaces in the analytic process. *International Journal of Psychoanalysis, 84*: 579–592.

Phillips, A. (1988). *Winnicott*. London: Fontana Modern Masters.

Plath, S. (1985). *Collected Poems*. London: Faber and Faber.

Plaut, A. (1966). Reflections on not being able to imagine. In: M. Fordham, R. Gordon, J. Hubback, K. Lambert, & M. Williams (Eds.), *Analytical Psychology: A Modern Science* (pp. 127–149). London: Heinemann, 1973.

Prodgers, A. (1991). On hating the patient. *British Journal of Psychotherapy*, 8(2): 144–153.

Quinodoz, D. (2003). Words that touch. *International Journal of Psychoanalysis*, 84: 1469–1485.

Renik, O. (1997). Reactions to "Observing–participation, mutual enactment, and the new classical models" by Irwin Hirsch, Ph.D. *Contemporary Psychoanalysis*, 33: 279–284.

Riviere, J. (1936). A contribution to the analysis of the negative therapeutic reaction. In: *The Inner World and Joan Riviere*. London: Karnac, 1991.

Rosenfeld, H. (1987). *Impasse and Interpretation*. London: Tavistock.

Rothstein, A. (1977). The ego attitude of entitlement. *International Review of Psycho-Analysis*, 4: 409–418.

Rusbridger, R. (2004). Elements of the Oedipus complex: a Kleinian account. *International Journal of Psychoanalysis*, 85: 731–747.

Sabbadini, A. (1991). Listening to silence. *British Journal of Psychotherapy*, 7(4): 406–415.

Sandler, J. (1976). Countertransference and role-responsiveness. *International Review of Psycho-Analysis*, 3: 43–47.

Schwaber, E. (1992). Countertransference: the analyst's retreat from the patient's vantage point. *International Journal of Psychoanalysis*, 73: 349–361.

Searles, H. (1959a). Oedipal love in the countertransference. In: *Collected Papers on Schizophrenia* (pp. 284–303). London: Hogarth Press, 1965.

Searles, H. (1959b). The effort to drive the other person crazy. *British Journal of Medical Psychology*, 32: 1–18.

Segal, H. (1957). Notes on symbol formation. *International Journal of Psychoanalysis*, 38: 391–397.

Slochower, J. (1991). Variations in the analytic holding environment. *International Journal of Psychoanalysis*, 72: 709–718.

Steiner, J. (1996). Revenge and resentment in the "Oedipus situation". *International Journal of Psychoanalysis*, 77: 433–443.

Steiner, J. (2006). Interpretative enactment and the analytic setting. *International Journal of Psychoanalysis*, 87: 315–320.

Stevenson, R. L. (1878). *El Dorado in Virginibus Puerisque and Other Papers*. London: Kegan Paul, 1881.

Stewart, H. (1990). Interpretation and other agents for psychic change. *International Journal of Psychoanalysis*, 71: 61–70.

Suttie, I. (1935). *The Origins of Love and Hate*. London: Free Association Books, 1988.

Symington, N. (1983). The analyst's act of freedom as agent of therapeutic change. *International Review of Psycho-Analysis, 10:* 283–291.

Tansey, M. (1994). Sexual attraction and phobic dread in the countertransference. *Psychoanalytic Dialogues, 4:* 139–152.

Tenzer, A. (1987). Grandiosity and its discontents. *Contemporary Psychoanalysis, 23:* 263–271.

Thomas, M. (2006). Absence and absent-mindedness. In: C. Harding (Ed.), *Aggression and Destructiveness* (pp. 221–236). London: Routledge.

Tuckett, D. (1997). Mutual enactment in the psychonalytic situation. In: J. Ahumada, et al. (Eds.), *The Perverse Transference and Other Matters: Essays in Honor of R. Horacio Etchegoyen* (pp. 203–216). New York and London: Jason Aronson.

Tustin, F. (1986). *Autistic Barriers in Neurotic Patients.* London: Karnac.

Tustin, F. (1990). *The Protective Shell in Children and Adults.* London: Karnac.

Welles, J. K., & Wrye, H. K. (1991). The maternal erotic countertransference. *International Journal of Psychoanalysis, 72:* 93–106.

Williams, P. (1998). "The theory of seduction and the problem of the other" by Jean Laplanche. *International Journal of Psychoanalysis, 79:* 205–210.

Winnicott, D. W. (1947). Hate in the countertransference. In: *Through Paediatrics to Psychoanalysis.* London: Hogarth, 1978.

Winnicott, D. W. (1950). Aggression in relation to emotional development. In: *Through Paediatrics to Psychoanalysis.* London: Hogarth, 1978.

Winnicott, D. W. (1952). Anxiety associated with insecurity. In: *Through Paediatrics to Psychoanalysis.* London: Hogarth, 1975.

Winnicott, D. W. (1956). Primary maternal preoccupation. In: *Through Paediatrics to Psychoanalysis.* London: Hogarth, 1975.

Winnicott, D. W. (1958). The capacity to be alone. In: *The Maturational Processes and the Facilitating Environment.* London: Hogarth, 1965.

Winnicott, D. W. (1960a). Ego distortion in terms of true and false self. In: *The Maturational Processes and the Facilitating Environment.* London: Hogarth Press, 1965.

Winnicott, D. W. (1960b). String: a technique of communication. In: *The Maturational Processes and the Facilitating Environment.* London: Hogarth, 1976.

Winnicott, D. W. (1963). Communicating and not communicating leading to a study of certain opposites. In: *The Maturational Processes and the Facilitating Environment.* London: Hogarth, 1976.

Winnicott, D. W. (1971). The use of an object and relating through identifications. In: *Playing and Reality*. London: Penguin.

Winnicott, D. W. (1974). Fear of breakdown. *International Review of Psycho-Analysis, 1*: 103–107.

Winston, A. (2009). Anorexia nervosa and the psychotherapy of absence. *British Journal of Psychotherapy, 25*: 77–90.

Wright, K. (1991). *Vision and Separation*. London: Free Association Books.

Wrye, H. K. (1993). Erotic terror: male patients' horror of the early maternal erotic transference. *Psychoanalytic Inquiry, 13*: 240–257.

Wrye, H. K., & Welles, J. K. (1989). The maternal erotic transference. *International Journal of Psychoanalysis, 70*: 673–684.

Yalom, I. D. (1991). *Love's Executioner*. London: Penguin.

INDEX